Talismans
& Amulets
of the World

Talismans & Amulets
of the World

Felicitas H. Nelson

Sterling Publishing Co., Inc
New York

Library of Congress Cataloging-in-Publication Data
Nelson, Felicitas H.
[Symbolsprache der Talismane Amulette. English]
Talismans& amulets of the world / Felicitas H. Nelson.
    p. cm.
Includes index.
ISBN 0-0869-2873-5
    1. Talismans. 2. Amulets. I. Title: Talismans and Amulets
of the world. II. Title.

GR600.N4413 2000
133.4'4—dc21

10 9 8 7 6 5 4 3 2

Published by Sterling Publishing Company, Inc.
387 Park Avenue South, New York, N.Y. 10016
First published in Germany
Under the title *Symbolsprache der Tailsmane Amulette*
and © 1998 by Schirner Verlag
English Translation © 2000 Sterling Publishing Co., Inc.
Distributed in Canada by Sterling Publishing
C/o Canadian Manda Group, One Atlantic Avenue, Suite 105
Toronto, Ontario, Canada M6K 3E7
Distributed in Great Britain and Europe by Cassell PLC
Wellington House, 125 Strand, London WC2R 0BB, England
Distributed in Australia by Capricorn Link (Australia) Pty Ltd.
P.O. Box 6651, Baulkham Hills, Business Centre, NSW 2153, Australia
Printed in Hong Kong
All rights reserved

Sterling ISBN 0-8069-2873-5

CONTENTS

The 12 Foundation Stones of Celestial Jerusalem　137

The Western Zodiac　151

Maya 165

Fetish Animals of the North American Southwest　189

Totem Spirits of the American Northwest　201

Power Animals　221

Talismans and Amulets from Various Cultures and Races　245

Index　269

FOREWORD

Since the beginning of time, human beings have worn objects that they have ascribed magical qualities. These objects were intended to protect their wearer from various outside forces; bring about certain events like love and happiness; or grant strength and enhance qualities that could be advantageous along life's journey. Even today, the very real attraction of such objects has lost none of its power. Talismans and amulets are like sheet anchors and they can be used to precipitate certain events. We humans live in a material world. Therefore, we require visible answers in order not to lose our faith and our trust. This has nothing to do with superstition, rather with our material nature.

This book presents a selection of ancient and modern talismans and amulets that are still available today. Almost every item described can be used either as a talisman or an amulet. To better tell them apart, one can make the following distinction: a talisman brings good luck, an amulet protects. It is possible to wear several talismans and amulets from different periods and cultures at the same time as long as they are used for different purposes. Each item should be used with only one intention.

I wish you love, happiness, success, and self-knowledge through wearing talismans and amulets. Live in peace and harmony!

Goddesses of Antiquity

VENUS - *Femininity*

Venus figurines date back some 25,000 years. They have been found from France to Asia. They embody the spiritual epiphany that can be achieved through sexual exercises, similar to tantric practices.

As a talisman it helps to:
- acknowledge the circle of birth, death, and rebirth
- experience the divine through sexuality
- give us an all-around healthy feeling toward our body

As an amulet it protects against:
- sexual harassment
- fear of one's own femininity
- frigidity

MOTHER GODDESSES - *Healing*

This goddess bears a woman in her lap whose arms are raised trustingly. She endows those who call on her with her powers to heal, as well as the power to teach the practice of secret knowledge.

As a talisman it helps to:
- recall long lost knowledge
- uncover secret truths and long buried mysteries
- regain one's health

As an amulet it protects against:
- illness and ignorance
- the rejection of spiritual truths
- exclusively rational thought and faith in technology

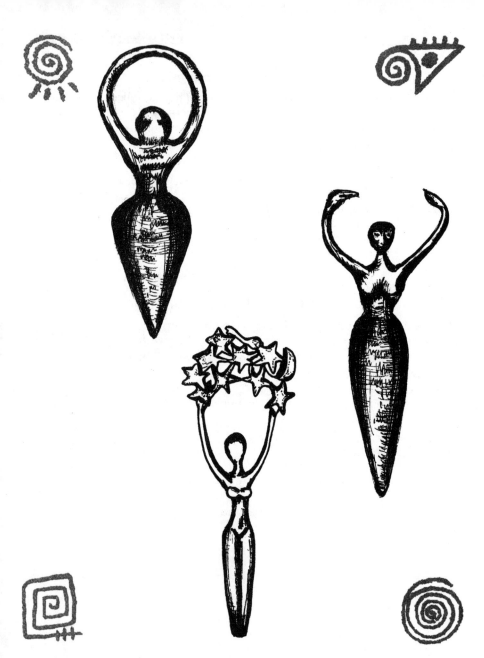

GAIA - *Earth Mother*

Uplifted arms form a circle above her headstand for harmony. The earth goddess joins all life on planet earth in this harmony. When we call on her for guidance, her wisdom teaches us to find our natural balance.

Helps as a talisman to:
- be in equilibrium with all life on earth
- regain physical, spiritual, and psychological balance
- develop grace and sight

Protects as an amulet against:
- environmental damages
- recklessness
- disturbances to equilibrium

GODDESS OF PROTECTION - *Warning*

Her raised arms warn us not to forget, in spite of our technologically regimented everyday life, who we really are and where we come from. Her form stands for the concentrated force that connects heaven and earth.

Helps as a talisman to:
- introduce ancient cultures and their customs into our daily lives
- remember our origins and to thereby gain energy in life

Protects as an amulet against:
- one's loss of roots
- disrespect of ancient customs
- machismo

ASTRAL GODDESS - *Dream*

She carries the stars in her hands, stretched high above her head. They glimmer and shine in the night sky and glide into our dreams. The goddess is the bearer of an ever-present dream state.

Helps as a talisman to:
- recall our dreams of the prior night
- move in our dreams through limitless spaces
- acknowledge in dreams another form of reality

Protects as an amulet against:
- restless sleep
- sleep-walking
- sleep without dreams

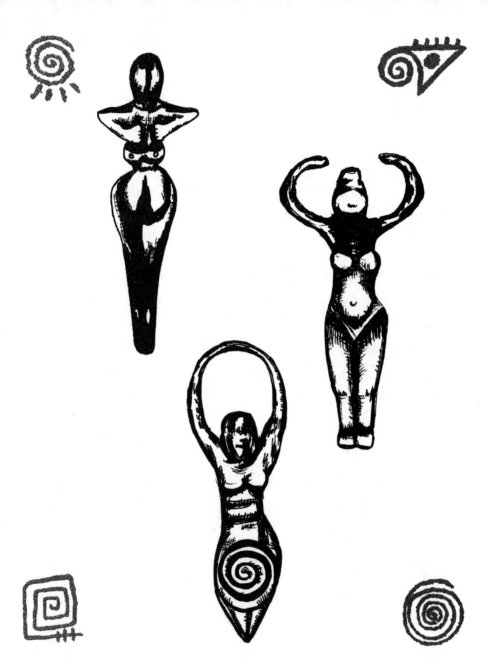

CYCLADIC GODDESS - *Patience*

3,000 years ago the power of this goddess was at its peak. The Cyclades are approximately 200 tiny islands between Crete and Turkey. Statues of this beautiful and powerful goddess in ritual poses were crafted there.

Helps as a talisman to:
- remain patient
- take time for our own rituals
- treat oneself to quiet breaks

Protects as an amulet against:
- stress and lack of time
- impatience and nerves

FALCON GODDESS - *Joy*

Strong, with powerful legs and arms raised like wings, this goddess is the feminine power of the spirit. She is the age-old dance of life, which teaches us to step lightly and spare the earth. She is the goddess of ancient times and of those to come.

Helps as a talisman to:
- float light as a bird over things
- attack as forcefully and proud as a falcon, if necessary
- feel the healing powers and joy of spirituality

Protects as an amulet against:
- bitterness
- passivity and weakness

GODDESS OF THE CIRCLE - *Affirmation*

This goddess dances in like a whirlwind. She has had many names throughout the ages: Gaia, the earth mother of the Greeks, Venus, Diana, Bona Dea, Inanna. She is unwavering proof of the spirit.

Helps as a talisman to:
- enjoy the circle of life
- be healed through dance
- be in possession of the spiritual present

Protects as an amulet against:
- depression
- circulatory ills
- interruptions during secular acts

GODDESS OF THE MOON RITUAL - *Peace*

The moon goddess leans with her back against the moon in a yoga position. She celebrates the moon ritual of peace and beauty. Her divine energy is real. Each ritual makes it more powerful. When we celebrate her ritual with each full moon, peace and beauty will follow. We are all a small part of our long-buried legacy.

Helps as a talisman to:
- organize our lives around the moon's phases
- be quiet and discrete
- bring out inner beauty

Protects as an amulet against:
- sleep disorders during a full moon
- aggression
- "overarching the bow"

GODDESS OF THE SPIRAL - *Creativity - Weaving*

The goddess of the spiral is constantly creating something new from herself. She reveals to us the goddess within ourselves, and makes us aware of our unique and creative visions in the world, helping us to realize them. We should take the risk of recognizing that we are the goddesses. We are the healers, and we ourselves weave the web of life.

Helps as a talisman to:
- realize new ideas
- stand behind one's own creations
- heal us through constant rejuvenation

Protects as an amulet against:
- low self-confidence
- feebleness and inertia
- inner emptiness

STONE AGE GODDESS - *Roots*

Many of these beautiful, delicate mother statuettes were made some 50,000 years ago. They point to one of our oldest religions. She holds her arms tightly wrapped around her body to recall the shape of a digging stick. Our ancestors used the stick in oldest times to remove roots from the earth for nourishment.

Helps as a talisman to:
- revitalize the past and to heal
- gain steadiness through one's own body
- always be collected

Protects as an amulet against:
- superficiality and too many interests
- unhealthy eating habits and their effects
- obesity and lack of discipline

BONA DEA - *Prediction*

She was the goddess of ancient Rome. No one knows her origins. Only women worshipped her, and only women were allowed into her ceremonies. Men faced the death penalty, if caught eavesdropping or spying. Even wives could not tell their husbands what went on. Bona Dea was also known as Fauna, "Good Goddess," or Fatua; the latter recalls fate, thus it is said that she bears the gift of prophecy.

Helps as a talisman to:
- be able to make prediction
- feel good among other women and to have the same aims
- be able to protect our household

Protects as an amulet against:
- patriarchy
- vanity for the sake of pleasing men
- hostility toward men

Egypt

UDJAT (UZAT, WADGET) - *Horus Eye - Healing*

The Horus Eye is the Protective Amulet.

The eye was one of the most important protective symbols in ancient Egypt. In this land of colors, nothing was as valuable to man as vision. The eye takes in one's surroundings but can also reproduce a person's many feelings and moods. Just think of the "flash of an eye."

The sun and the moon are the eyes of the falcon god Horus. The right eye is the sun, the left the moon. The right eye stands for activity, and the future; the left for passivity, and the past. Both eyes together stand for clear-sightedness at day or night. This is the reason the Horus eye has been associated with omnipotence. Invulnerability and eternal fruition are also linked to the eye. They were often placed on the left-hand side of the sarcophagus so that the dead could find their way.

On the large amulet illustrated below, two suns from Karneol are represented along with the Horus sun. For the Egyptians, Karneol was one of the most divine stones and directly connected to the sun.

Helps as a talisman to:
- maintain good health and revitalize oneself
- achieve or to increase fertility and creative potentials
- see others heart-to-heart

Protects as an amulet against:
- the evil eye
- blindness

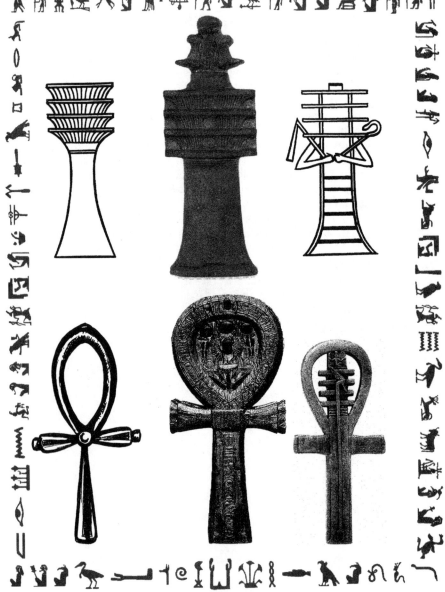

DJED COLUMN - *Spine of Osiris - Resurrection*

Before the Egyptian age, the Djed column was a fetish item that probably depicted a pole that grain had been piled around. It symbolized a cult of fertility. The power of grain and its renewed growth was thereby stimulated. This makes it the general symbol for "duration."

In the late empire the Djed column became a symbol of Osiris, the god of resurrection who stands for fertility and eternal duration. The Djed column became the spinal column of the god. The column represents the victory of Osiris over his nemesis Seth.

The dead were given the Djed column as an amulet, and one often finds these items where the spine of the mummy lies. The amulet should bring about the resurrection of the dead, allowing his life to be eternal, and his fertility to be undiminished.

ANKH - *Looped cross - Life*

This symbol is still a riddle even today. As a hieroglyph it signifies "life" and connotes the eternal, divine life. It was once a sexual symbol, which was brought into connection with intransigence, air, and water. It appears whenever the gods give the gift of life or the life-breath to the king by holding the Ankh cross before his nose. We also find the fertilization of the earth by the sun; the sun, represented by the highest sphere, the earth by the lowest cross. The looped cross often appears held by the gods on a ring, making it the key that unlocks the realm of the dead.

The Ankh symbol is one of the most powerful amulets in ancient Egypt. Its power gives us eternal life and fertility. In connection with the Djed column (illustration, far right) the Ankh cross symbolizes the union of masculine and feminine principles for the purpose of propagation. Masculine challenge (creative powers, below: Tau cross of Osiris) and feminine opening of oneself (fertility, above: Oval of Isis) merge here to form a union that gives birth to new life.

SCHEN RING - *Eternity*

The kneeing figure in the adjoining illustration is touching a ring with her hands. The ring has neither beginning nor end and thus, embodies infinity. Like almost all round motives, it also originates from the sun. This type of ring, whose ends are bound like knots on a slip string, is known as a magic ring. It protects against illness and other evils.

BASTET - *Cat Goddess - Protector*

The cat Bastet was first associated with the sun. Male cats were thought to embody the sun god, female cats the eye of the sun. Since the Middle Empire the house cat was assigned to the goddess Bastet. This goddess took on more tender characteristics in the late empire. She came to be associated with the moon. The image of the cat changed, and only the large cat came to be associated with the sun; the house cat was associated with the moon, hence with the unconscious and the feminine. It became the protector of the house, of mothers, and of children.

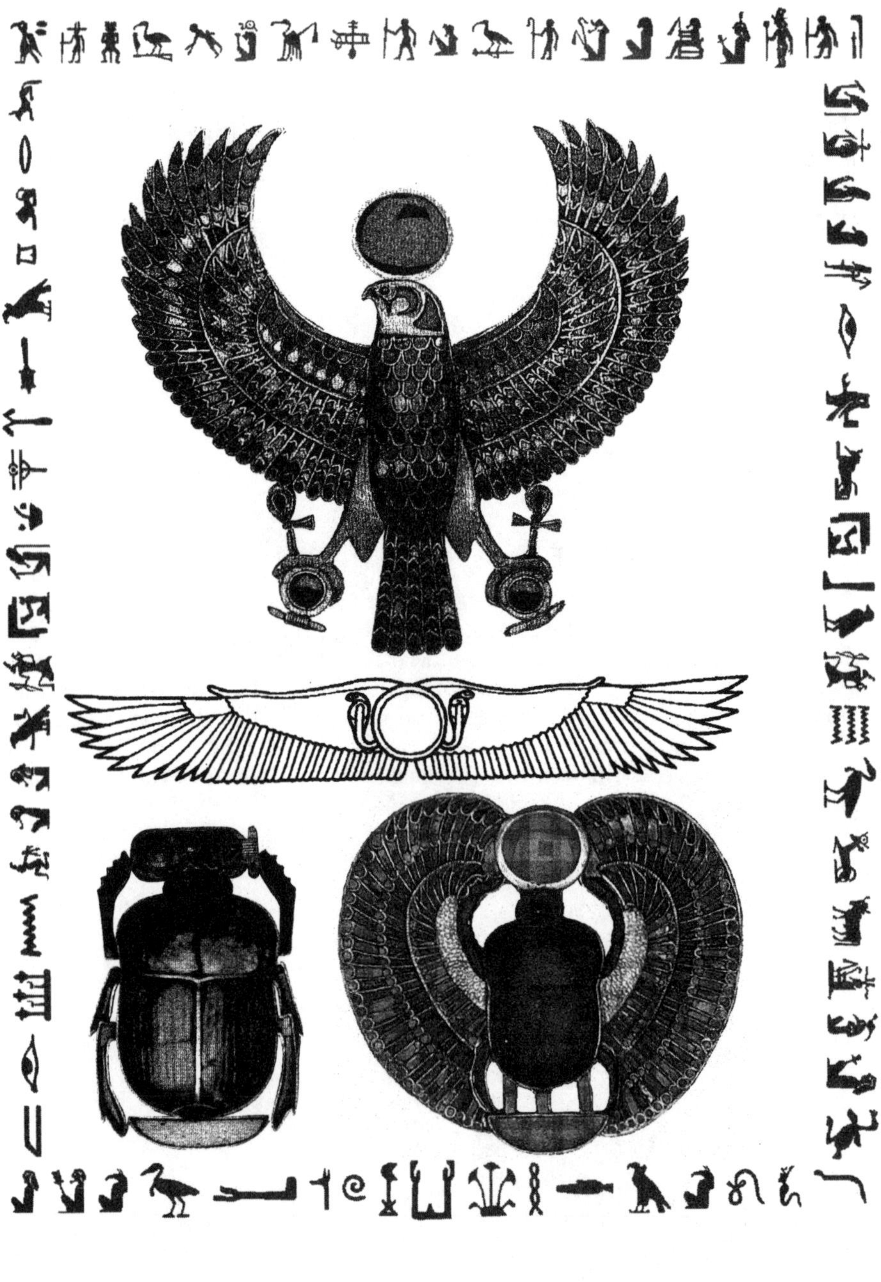

FALCON - *God* - *Protection*

The falcon shown on the adjoining page bears the Schen Ring and Ankh Cross in both claws. It wears the red sun of Karneol on its head. The falcon was highly esteemed for its agility in flight and for its aggressiveness. It was known as the "King of the Air" and became a symbol for "god." With its wings spread, it flies between the sun and the earth, thus protecting all creatures in heaven and on earth.

A somewhat more abstract representation or a shorter form can be seen in the image of the sun with wings. This example shows how varied the Egyptians' depictions of the sun were and points to the important status of such images in their thought. In the late empire, the sun was given a different form at each time of day and even at each hour, for example, as child, crocodile, falcon, lion, or griffin.

SCARAB - *The Holy Dung Beetle*

Creator from out of itself

The scarab was the most popular good luck charm in ancient Egypt. It has many different forms. On the left, we see it with a royal cartridge between its front legs; on the right, it takes the form of the sun god Chepre (i.e., he who has risen from the earth), the symbol of new life. It became the symbol of the sun, which the ancient Egyptians believed was walked or rolled across the sky, by the Scarab, because the insect often was found rolling a ball of dirt in front of itself, in which its eggs lay. When the time is right, new scarabs emerge from the dung: new life has arisen from the earth, signifying rebirth.

The I-Ching

TAI-CHI- *The "One"- The Last Thing*

The Original Beginning

This ancient symbol of the Taoists shows the male and female principles uniting and merging with each other. This dichotomy gives birth to everything. Lao Tse and Chuang Tzu founded the school of Taoism in the 4th century BC Its aim was to "join effortlessly with the dualistic principle that governs the universe." The Yin-Yang symbol is well known to most Westerners. It appears again and again in art, graphics, and even advertising. This symbol has an eternal value. The Chinese say: "The creative Yin and the receptive Yang allow the ten thousand things to exist." Wear this ancient Chinese amulet to protect your inner harmony and to stimulate personal growth.

TAI-CHI ENCIRCLED BY 8 TRIGRAMS

Out of the great whole, which is divided into light and dark, everything arises and each part carries the other as its seed in itself, building thereby its extension. This good luck charm is found on the back of I-Ching talismans. The image illustrates how the one is made by the other and from whence it comes. Nothing stands alone.

This talisman assists us on the way to self-knowledge and helps us to meditate on all existence. As an amulet, it keeps us from overestimating ourselves and shows us our proper place.

I-KIEN - *Creativity*

Resolution and indefatigable strength

This character shows the sun on the left, shining through the plants. On the right, the first impulse from the sun takes root. Of the two male trigrams, the "heavens" exerts the strongest pull, the pervasive power of life.

Helps as a talisman to:
- gain leadership positions and success by means of creative powers and aggressiveness
- strive for meaningful goals and take over the leadership role in the family

Protects as an amulet against:
- excessive difficulties
- aimlessness, distractions, and meaninglessness
Assignation: May

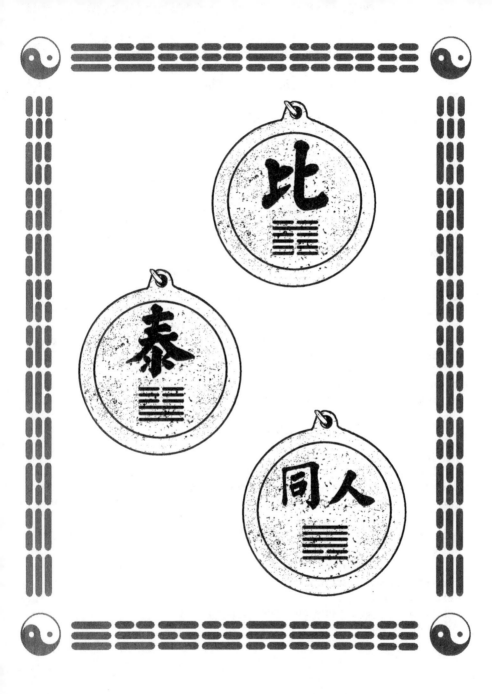

8-BI - *Unity: Mutual Assistance*

Two people stand side by side and glance to the right, which is into the future. Their proximity points to their shared feelings, thoughts, and actions. The trigram below "earth" is covered by the trigram "water," as it was on earth in ancient times. That is the unity out of which life develops.

Helps as a talisman to:
- recognize the proper moment and act accordingly
- reevaluate one's own authority again and again

Protects as an amulet against:
- self-righteousness and tardiness
Assignation: September

11-TAI - *Peace*

Working together and internal harmony

A superior person is able to work his or her field with both hands in peace and harmony. The upper trigram "earth" sinks to below, the lower trigram "sky" rises to above. Thus they merge with one another and achieve inner harmony, which makes life blossom. This symbol can be a good luck charm.

Helps as a talisman to:
- improve the present situation
- begin new relationships and develop new powers and become healthy

Protects as an amulet against:
- conflict, mistrust, money problems, and illness
Assignation: February-March

13-TUNG JEN - *Joy*

Belonging and brotherly community. A man stands beside a pot tightly sealed by a lid. The lower trigram "fire" climbs toward the air (upper trigram, the sky). Everything is as it must be. Two different powers join together, to face adversity better.

Helps as a talisman to:
- renounce all personal desire and to prepare oneself for the new and strange
- risk new undertakings to create order from chaos

Protects as an amulet against:
- envy and ill-will - personal interests - animosity toward strangers
Assignation: July

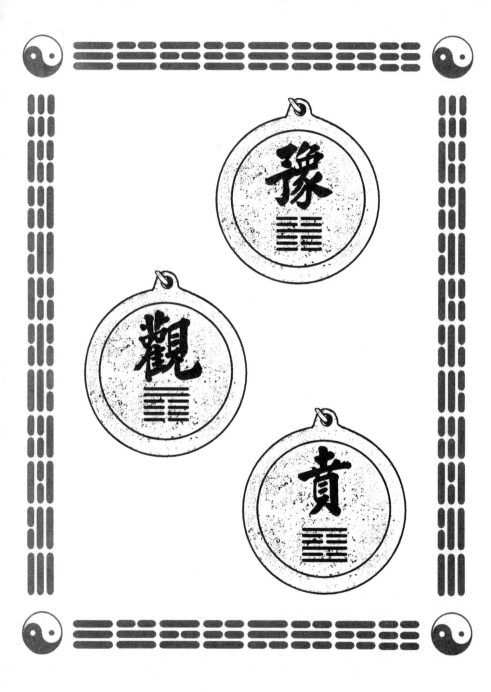

16-YU - *Enthusiasm*

The balance between the head and the heart. Two rackets touch each other on the left, indicating a peaceful exchange. On the right stands an elephant, the symbol of majesty. The encounter as a whole has an honorable appearance. From the earth below, the thunder climbs and mingles with mankind. This is how tension is expelled and enthusiasm grasps everyone, players as well as spectators.

Helps as a talisman to:
- follow one's inner voice- go the way of least resistance - ground oneself in the present and to follow one's biological rhythm to a healthy way of life

Protects as an amulet against:
- unfounded hopes - the loss of internal drive - obstinacy
Assignation: March

20-GUAN - *Observation*

Recognition of the divine order. A magnificent, stern bird calls to the person beside him, who looks back at him. The person, is observed by a giant eye. The upper trigram "wind" blow across the earth and forms a giant tower. In Taoism, GUAN embodies the "art of feeling."

Helps as a talisman to:
- act through inaction (Wu Wei) - be complete in the moment - have influence - practice objective self-knowledge

Protects as an amulet against:
- narrow horizons - prejudices - superficial observations and egotism
Assignation: September- October

22-BI - *Grace*

This symbol shows an oyster below as decoration. Below, the fire smolders and illuminates the mountain so that it shimmers with beauty. Beauty is important for this union because it allows it to unfold in an orderly fashion.

Helps as a talisman to:
- bring good luck to those who seek a great profit in business - unite beauty
Protects as an amulet against:
- everything ugly and coarse - judging the inner by the outer
Assignation: August

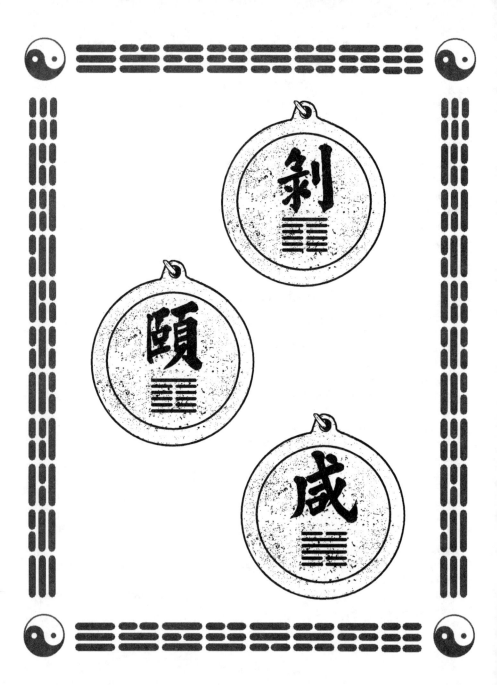

23-BO - *Division*

Generosity pays off. Someone is climbing a tree whose branches have been cut off by an ax. He is also whittling an arrow. The dark earth rises to carve out the mountain. If we come together time reveals the truth to us. This symbol is the equivalent of the "Hanged Man" in the tarot.

Helps as a talisman to:
- reaffirm life's basics - give patience and goodwill toward others - keep calm in personal relations and to act generously

Protects as an amulet against:
- despair - hurried action at the wrong moment
Assignation: October-November

27-I - *Nutrition*

One is what one eats. Left: there is a face in profile. Right: it faces us. Chewing and swallowing are symbolized here. The thunder is below, the mountain, above: together they form the stripe of an open mouth across the picture. The lower part represents one's own nutrition, the upper care for others, including the spiritual.

Helps as a talisman to:
- stay healthy through nutrition - the correct relation between spiritual and physical nutrition - fulfill the needs of others

Protects as an amulet against:
- out of control eating habits - ingestion of bad and loss of good - greed
Assignation: November

31-HIEN - *Attraction*

The basis of all social relations. Filled with happiness, a figure strides toward something with outstretched arms. The lower trigram is the younger man, the upper the younger woman. Both of them need to move toward one another. This is the attraction of the sexes.

Helps as a talisman to:
- be open to all things in life - spontaneously enter into a relationship that ends in marriage

Protects as an amulet against:
- loneliness and bitterness - unhealthy addictions - gullibility
Assignation: June

34- DA DSCHUANG - *The Great Power*

Perseverance is Divine. On the left, there is a powerful person with arms spread. On the right, there is an upright tree, which symbolizes strength, and a wise old man, who doles out advice. The lower star sign points to and supports the thunder above. Inner worth comes to fruition. One should not rely solely on one's own powers but, instead, constantly question these powers.

Helps as a talisman to:
- remain just and righteous - find power and responsibility - improve relations and to assume the leadership role

Protects as an amulet against:
- bragging and pride - the entropy of a standstill - powerlessness
Assignation: March - April

37-GIA JEN - *The Family*

The Perseverance of Woman is Divine. The pig is inside the barn. Beside him, there is a member of this family. The wife has to make sure that everything is in order. She is depicted in the scene. The lower trigram "fire" produces warmth in the house. Outside it controls the wind.

Helps as a talisman to:
- remain faithful and act now - support those whose respect can further oneself - find one's proper place in life, fulfill one's duties, and reach one's goals

Protects as an amulet against:
- the risk of going alone - irresponsibility - the loss of family traditions

38-KUI - *The Opposite*

Fire and water. During the day, different people meet at a table. They don't all agree but there isn't a major conflict. Differences make changes possible, and varied opinions place the ordinary in a new light. The upper symbol "fire" flares up, and the lake below runs down. The movement strives to divide, but opposites build harmony in creation.

Helps as a talisman to:
- disregard a passing discrepancy - conquer evil - differentiate between good and evil

Protects as an amulet against:
- false and careless actions - unambiguous division

2-1 - *Profit*

Past acts come to fruition. An overflowing vessel, filled with fluid, stands on the ground. The thunder and wind whip themselves into a storm and offer an image of reproduction. A time of great prosperity is coming. Decisions must be made. The time is ripe.

Helps as a talisman to:
- win in games - replace old habits and gain new ones - acquire great wealth

Protects as an amulet against:
- complacency - missing an opportunity - egotism
Assignation: January

43-GUAI - *Decisiveness*

Obstacles are overcome A large hand holds a rake, which is opening the earth with total determination. The sky below rises up to dispel the water above and make it beautiful again. All the power of a single threatening cloud is thus dispersed.

Helps as a talisman to:
- find solutions - keep a clear head and to master difficult situations - trust people close to you and thereby to be rewarded

Protects as an amulet against:
- hate and unbridled passions - pride and unjustified self-confidence
Assignation: April

44-GOU - *Meetings*

On the right a prince is bowing over a barrel. To the left stands a strong girl who is trying to sway him. The dark trigram "wind" tries to press upwards and gain power.

Helps as a talisman to
- bring favorable results in social and business meetings
- bring one's will into agreement with the larger context
- mistrust unexpected meetings and through one's proper conduct to make the wished for meetings

Protects as an amulet against:
- a rushed marriage - temptation - carelessness
Assignation: June-July

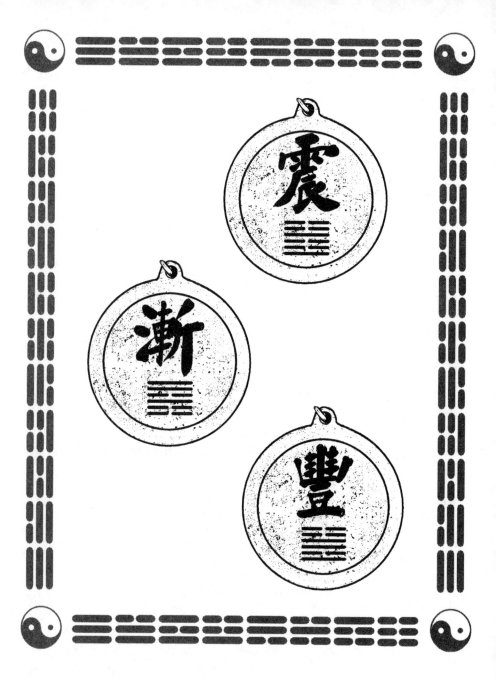

51-DSCHEN - *Thunder/Excitement*

Success is on the way. A person bowed down in fear is overc
der and lightning. Having withstood the storm, the relief is great. The two
trigrams depict "thunder" at the peak of its chaos. It is the power of nature;
whoever keeps calm enjoys a cleansed nature afterwards.

Helps as a talisman to:
- overcome fear and keep everything in perspective - laugh even in the face
of terror - act with power and bring success

Protects as an amulet against:
- terrifying others - freezing in moments of danger - overestimating oneself

53-DSIEN - *Development*

Step by step we come closer to our goal. This symbol shows a river bed
buried after millions of years. While the person on the right is working the
earth, a heavily laden wagon fights its way forward,. In the lowest trigram,
the mountain carries the woods, which grows and has a solid background;
the sun frees itself from the earth and lifts itself up into the sky. This all
reveals an ordered environment where everything follows according to plan.

Helps as a talisman to:
- act calmly and methodically, never losing sight of one's plan - be honored
for generosity - bring about a well-planned marriage and fidelity - exist in
harmony with one's surroundings

Protects as an amulet against:
- haste, which causes defeat - impermanence and passion, which bring about
suffering
Assignation: January

55-FONG - *Fulfillment*

Two cornstalks are a sacrifice in the ritual vessel. The harvest has been
unusually good. We can give without fear of hunger. But,there is the wish
that the coming harvest will be just as rich. Above the fire trigram one finds
the "thunder." We can accomplish more than we imagined. It couldn't be
better. We should use the time because the uncertain future is approaching.

Helps as a talisman to:
- enjoy the moment - be free of worry - realize dreams with a real partner

Protects as an amulet against:
- stinginess and thus loneliness - self-profit - helplessness

56-LU - *The Traveler: The Journey through Life*

A large person is protecting two people seeking shelter. In the lower trigram, one finds the mountain, immobile since the beginning of time. The fire on the mountain burns for only one night; the travelers move on, leaving each other. By changing our companions, we can change our position.

Helps as a talisman to:
- undertake a journey and not postpone it - persevere and gain knowledge - ask modestly for and receive help

Protects as a talisman
- evil on a voyage - bad accommodations and poor company

58-DUI - *Happiness: Joy and Courage*

This symbol shows the throat and a shorn head. The mouth is speaking in the center. This speech is divided into two parts on the upper half of the image. If one insists on one's due, the sought after will be attained. Success and happiness will follow. The trigram depicts the lake twice; it is a symbol of happiness, which is tender and mild on the outside, but firm inside without allowing itself to be misled.

Helps as a talisman to:
- encourage others - be faithful and work together through inner knowledge and outer cheer - be able to share important things with others

Protects as an amulet against:
- exaggerated indifference - frivolity - intimidation

59-HUAN - *The Reunion: The Elimination of Dangers*

A man stands on a roof. Two hands reach up to him. On the left, there is a river, the symbol of being carried away. The water (lower trigram) is dispersed by the wind; the flood will soon end. One can approach the evil together, in order to dispel it. Unity provides stability.

Helps as a talisman to:
- disperse old differences of opinion and conflicts - set free blocked energies - renew contact with one's relations in order to attain strength

Protects as an amulet against:
- irreconcilable differences - being turned down - disbelief in others' abilities
Assignation: June

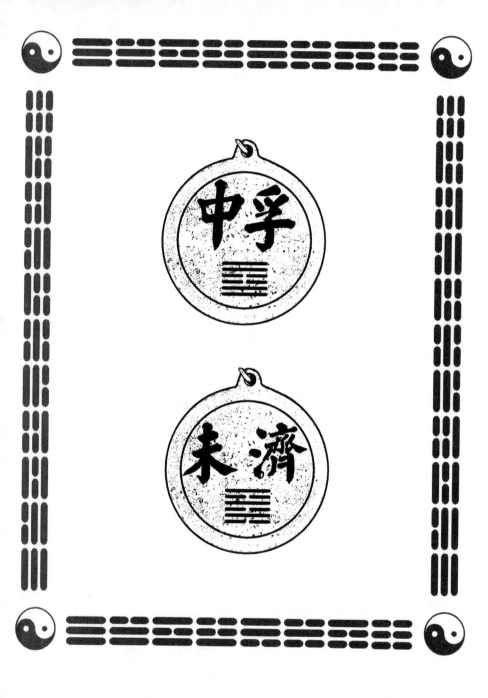

DSCHUNG FU - *The Inner Truth*

The Choice of the Right Way. The arrow pierces the center of the disk, symbolizing the inner, the harmonic. A bird nests on the right; a claw floats above, protecting the sobbing boy. Mutual trust and commitment to duty is the highest inner truth. Above the lake (lower trigram) the wind blows (upper trigram). In the center, the symbol is open; the heart is free from being caged.

Helps as a talisman to:
- establish meaningful relations, in order to reach common goals
- attain insight into profound truths
- lead a healthy life

Protects as an amulet against:
- deception
- lack of a sense of reality
- being misled and unreliability
Assignation: November

64-WE DSI - *Before Completion*

Uncertainty is dissolved. A very large tree grows without respite. Beside it, there flows a river on which perfection already stands. In the near future the conclusion will take place. But obstacles and errors can still arise. Make this your motto: one should not praise the day before the evening. We should, at this point, be on the watch, not celebrating too early. The trigram "fire" over the trigram "water" shows the transition from chaos to order.

Helps as a talisman to:
- raise hope for a happy end
- be wary and persist
- overcome obstacles

Protects as an amulet against:
- the violent pressure of a conclusion
- spontaneous, unplanned decisions
- depression
Assignation: December

The Chinese Zodiac

RAT - *Profit (1924, 1936, 1948, 1960, 1972, etc.)*

The rat's incisors are quite visible in this illustration; so is his long tail. The rat is constantly seeking to increase its possessions and secure its well being. It's fear of hunger and poverty is great. But it also loves pleasure and can throw it all away for love.

Helps as a talisman to:
- succeed in politics and business
- develop passion and feelings
- sense good opportunities and be able to enjoy them

Protects as an amulet against:
- blind faith
- volubility
- lack of ideas

BUFFALO - *Patience (1925, 1937, 1949, 1961, 1973, etc.)*

The buffalo is a hoofed animal, tamed by man to provide services. Whoever owns a buffalo enriches his home and family. The buffalo is sedentary, persistent and powerful. It attacks its goals with lowered horns.

Helps as a talisman to:
- develop a sense of precision and joy at work
- strengthen a sense of tradition
- appear trustworthy and serious

Protects as an amulet against:
- fashionable tomfoolery
- infidelity
- poverty and insecurity

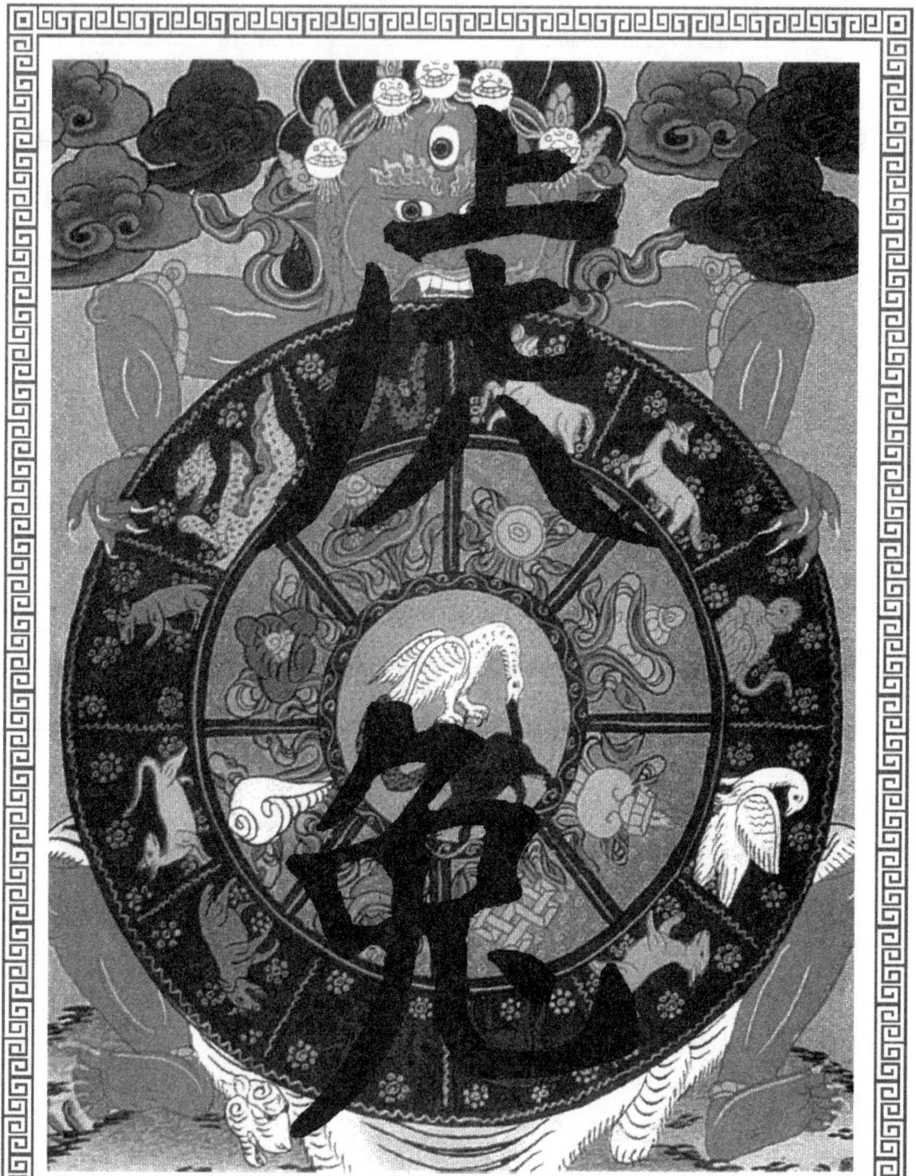

TIGER - *Daring (1926, 1938, 1950, 1962, 1974, etc.)*

The tiger slips in graceful and powerful, with a long tail. Its beauty strikes down everyone. Its character as a beast of prey gives it the right to lay claim to its prize for itself alone. For the tiger, human laws do not apply.

Helps as a talisman to:
- take risks and finally dare something
- experience adventures in love
- attract luck

Protects as an amulet against:
- dangers in the home caused by other people or by nature
- injustice
- subjugation

RABBIT - *Beauty (1927, 1939, 1951, 1963, 1975, etc.)*

We know the rabbit from its big, beautiful eyes and delicate ears. Its long legs and rather bushy tail make it seem quiet and withdrawn. It needs to be pampered. The rabbit is self-contained and isn't really interested in the problems or suffering of others.

Helps as a talisman to:
- make oneself beloved by others and establish respect
- attract beauty and love
- lead a long, fun life

Protects as an amulet against:
- ignorance
- a lack of tact and indiscretion
- carelessness

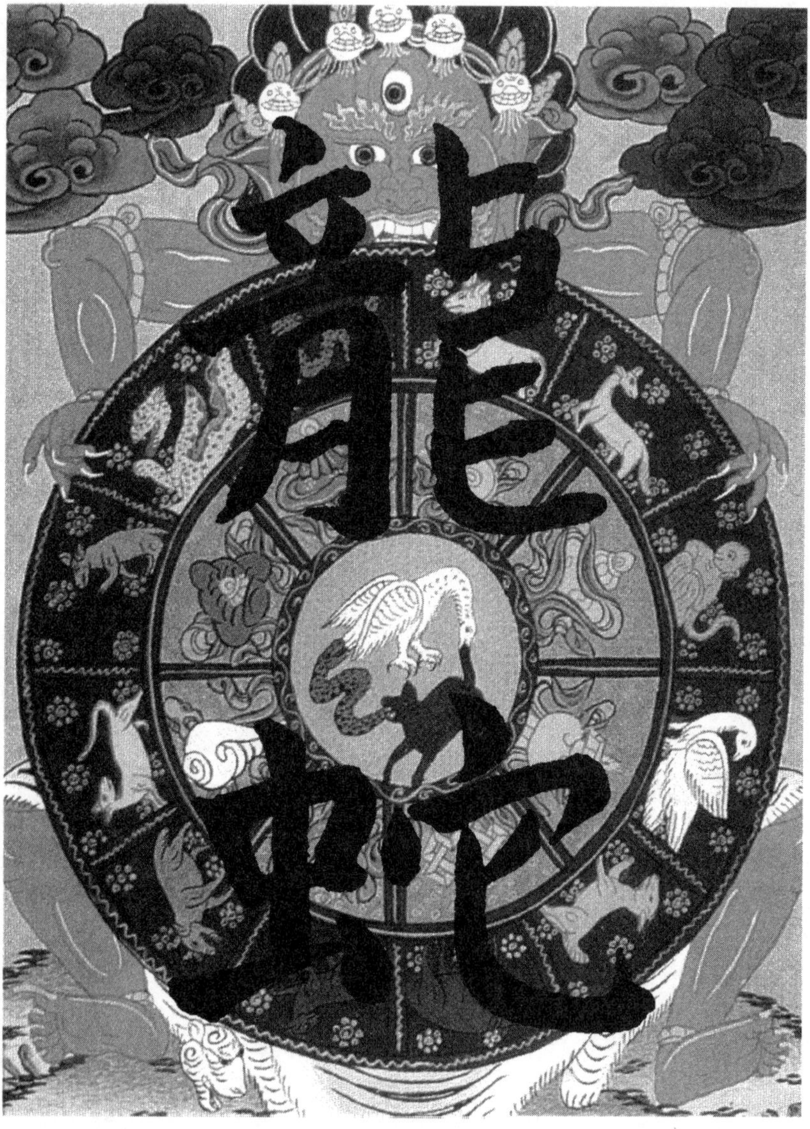
龍
蛇

DRAGON - *Influence (1928, 1940, 1952, 1964, 1976, etc.)*

The fiery sun gave birth to the dragon with his long, spiked tail. This is the reason he spews fire and glides in gracious waving motions through the clouds. He is trying to make a big impression, but sometimes his aim is off the mark. It's easy to see that often, it's just hot air that inflates him.

Helps as a talisman to:
- overcome all effort with will power
- exert a great influence
- attract good luck in love and matters of the heart

Protects as an amulet against:
- hypocrisy
- money woes
- the desire for constant company

SNAKE - *Intelligence (1929, 1941, 1953, 1965, 1977, etc.)*

With its hypnotic gaze, the snake draws its enemies into its power. Its body and tail wriggle in a strange motion and can also embrace and wrap up, even smother. Its scales shine with the brightest of colors. It knows what it wants.

Helps as a talisman to:
- increase will power
- develop wit, char,m and cleverness
- promote intuition and clairvoyance

Protects as an amulet against:
- illness and disease
- hesitation and indecisiveness
- waste and having to give up something (money or a partner)

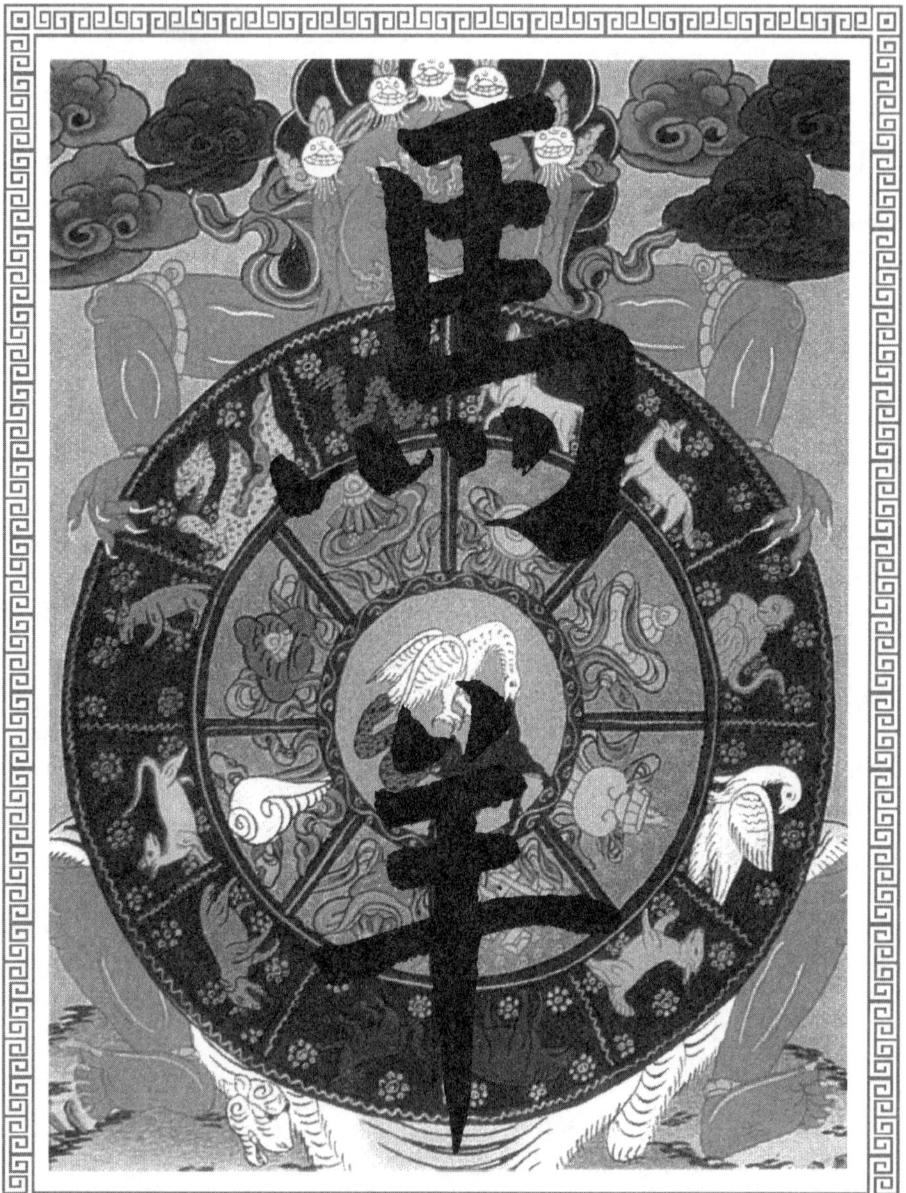
马年

HORSE - *Speed (1930, 1942, 1954, 1966, 1978, etc.)*

The horse gallops on four hooves; its mane blows in the wind. It is strong and noble. The horse has the ability to act quickly. The horse feels best outdoors, in nature, where it can really live. Or, when someone cleans its stall and prepares its food.

Helps as a talisman to:
- practice a special sport
- enhance a language aptitude and to convince an opponent
- develop independence

Protects as an amulet against:
- unpopularity
- financial difficulties
- one-dimensionality

GOAT - *Talent (1931, 1943, 1955, 1967, 1979, etc.)*

The goat is also a domesticated animal with hooves. Its horns leap out from its skull and can be very imposing. The goat leaps hurdles with ease, but its timing is unpredictable. If you tie a goat down, expect to put up with its grousing. The goat loves to have others assume responsibility.

Helps as a talisman to:
- receive advice
- engage in the occult sciences
- develop a readiness to help out others

Protects as an amulet against:
- change or disturbances to one's lifestyle
- responsibility
- thinking possessively and striving for material goods

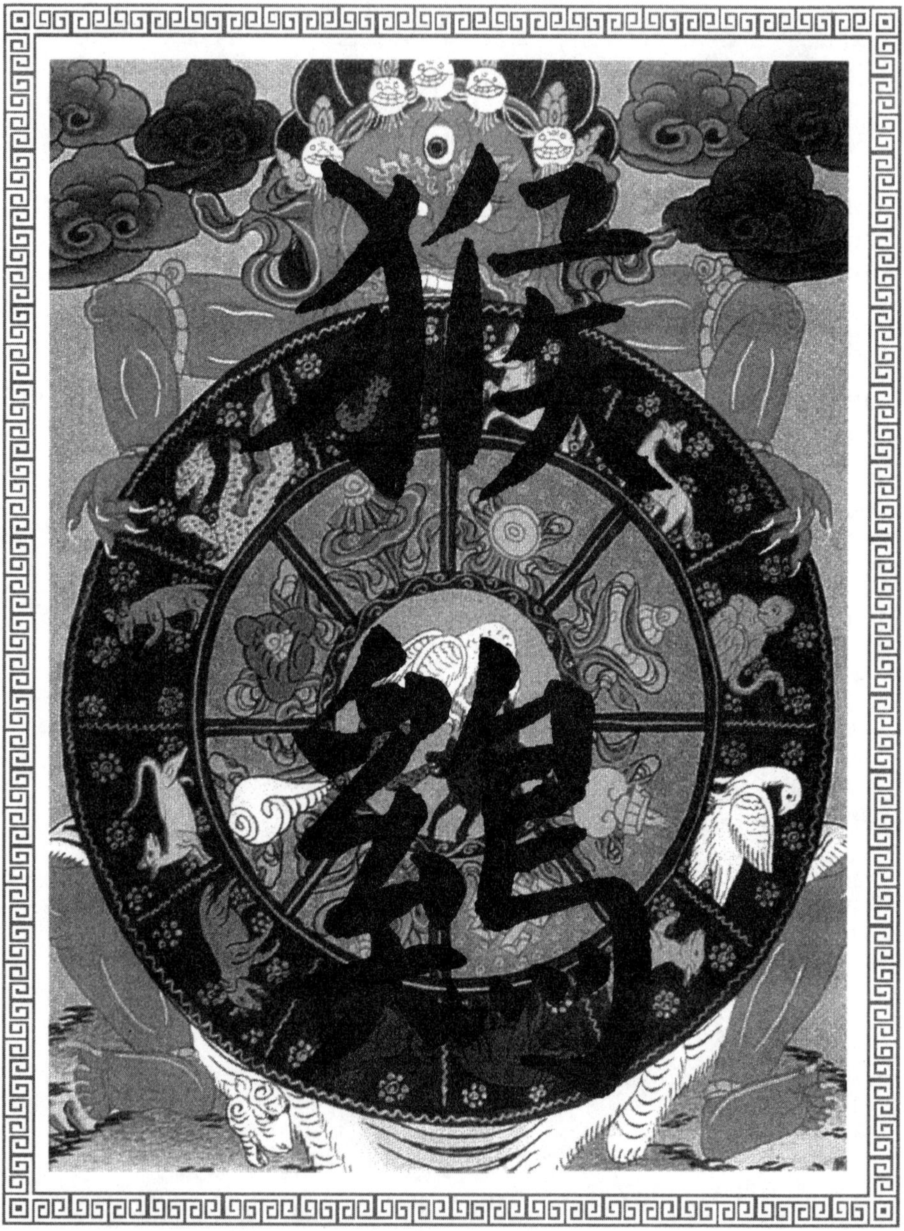

MONKEY - *Humor (1932, 1944, 1956, 1968, 1980, etc.)*

With legs spread and sitting almost like a human, the monkey plays around in the air. Its movements are inconsistent, and its interests constantly shifting. He tries to cleverly keep himself out of affairs and intrigues, often making fools of others.

Helps as a talisman to:
- live out one's desire for knowledge through study and reading
- immediately solve difficult problems
- deal diplomatically and adeptly
- be able to laugh at one's own mistakes

Protects as an amulet against:
- lapses of conscience
- depression (protects with humor)
- homogeneity and boredom of life

ROOSTER - *Boldness (1933, 1945, 1957, 1969, 1981, etc.)*

The rooster, with its plume of feathers and puffed out chest, is the lord of the chicken yard. He is the first to greet the morning and quickly gets to work. The rooster diligently spreads his spores and even gets into a fight now and then; but what he likes best is to sit with his chickens and boast about his adventures.

Helps as a talisman to:
- speak directly and to the point
- act with courage and to be a good fighter
- be content with one's work in spite of dreams

Protects as an amulet against:
- laziness
- sheer braggadocio
- blandness and predictability

DOG - *Vigilance (1934, 1946, 1958, 1970, 1982, etc.)*

Warily, and with ears perked the dog creeps around the house. Sometimes it chases off unwelcome guests. The dog heeds his master's word, because he wants to instill trust.

Helps as a talisman to:
- maintain vigilance, keep alert
- enhance fidelity and a sense of duty
- instill trust and to be valued
- reach your goal through persistence

Protects as an amulet against:
- betrayal and distrust
- injustice
- material ballast

PIG - *Cheeriness (1935, 1947, 1959, 1971, 1983, etc.)*

This animal likes best to live in close proximity to people, who will sometimes scratch his round back. The pig is good-natured and delights in pleasure. Its motto is: live and let live.

Helps as a talisman to:
- be tolerant and sensitive
- not take sides or make compromises, but to deal fairly
- be happy in company and to enjoy life

Protects as an amulet against:
- deception and betrayal
- being argumentative and dishonest
- conflicts and disputes

The Celts

THE SUN GOD - *Light of Life*

The burning sun was portrayed as a man in almost all ancient cultures. Flames leap from the face of the sun god, Suli, and look like hair. Our modern-day idea of god is based on this depiction of a genial god who is omnipotent and omnipresent. The druids carried this signet over their hearts.

Helps as a talisman to:
- be in tune with the joy of life
- feel self-confident
- keep a sunny outlook

Protects as an amulet against:
- physical and spiritual weakness

THE CELTIC WHEEL - *Spiritual Power*

The Celtic Wheel is one of the world's original symbols. It can be found in the medicine wheel of the North American Native Americans. The wheel symbolizes infinity without beginning or end. The cross stands for the visible, tangible world, its four compass points, the four elements, the four times of day, the four phases of the moon, the four seasons. Four is the number of stability, the eternally same. In the middle of the wheel, one finds the original force from which physical and spiritual vitality pours forth into the world.

Helps as a talisman to:
- receive spiritual power from the origin
- be firm in all actions
- extend one's effects in all directions
- go the way of wisdom and self-knowledge

PICTIC KNOTS (VALKNUTR) - *Eternal Change*

The knots of the chosen ones embody the new worlds in the three realms, which are bound together in eternal unity. The knots bring out the eternal powers of the universe: birth, death, rebirth. This signet is worn as an amulet.

Protects as an amulet against:
- petty motivations
- mistakes in the practice of magic rites
- dangers in general

THE TRISKEL (TRIADIC SPIRAL) - *Devotion*

Once again, we come across a triadic symbol, which contains smaller spirals within its larger spirals. This is the dancing wheel of creation. Its spinning energy flows through all life. The ancient Celts used this sign as protection against misfortune and for the complete repulsion of all evil.

Helps as a talisman to:
- fulfill the heart's desire, if placed under one's pillow
- nurture inner wisdom and devotion to life
- completely change oneself, spiritually as well as physically

CELTIC TRIANGLE KNOTS - *Inspiration*

This symbol illustrates that the Celts did not express religious ideas in images. Their profound knowledge took the form of geometric figures, like knots, spirals, and labyrinths. Once again we are looking at a triadic symbol, which signifies the union of body, mind, and soul. The twists and turns of the figure represent the turns on the path of life.

Helps as a talisman to:
- develop intuition
- listen closely to inspiration
- unite the inner with the outer

Protects as an amulet against:
- one-dimensional lifestyles
- a lack of fantasy
- the belief that life is a straight path

CELTIC KNOTS WITH THREE HORSES- Power

The horse in the Celtic tradition is one of the most important power animals. It belongs to the goddess Epona and is a symbol of power, endurance, and beauty. The triadic construction expresses the balance between body, mind, and spirit. It also points to the triadic nature of the sacred. Warriors wore this symbol for protection in battle.

Helps as a talisman to:
- enter into battle (work or debate) with courage
- be in harmony with body, mind, and spirit
- be aware of one's daily life
- maintain a balance with the divine

Protects as an amulet against:
- imbalances
- cowardliness
- anxieties

THE FOURFOLD CELTIC KNOT - *Intuition*

These knots show the interwoven nature of the universe. Everything is connected, even when it doesn't seem so at first glance. Hidden paths must be followed in order to comprehend the world of the body and spirit. The Celts understood the number four to be a doubling of the number two and to be bound with the "lunar" (moon). It also demonstrates the extension of space. For instance, in the two adjoining illustrations, the four points jut out beyond the wheel of life. The talisman on the left shows the windings of the unconscious, which expresses itself as intuition. The right-hand image stands for the vitality that pours forth from the center into the outside world, where it is experience as a powerful emanation.

Helps as a talisman
- (left) to develop intuition
- (right) to live up to one's fullest powers

CIRCLES WITH CELTIC KNOTS - *Love and Friendship*

Both circles are aligned with the moon, that is, with the unconscious. They are shaped around the number two, thus are best applied to couples, feelings, and passion. They both have the same effect.

Helps as a talisman to:
- attract and exude love
- be one with the beloved
- become friends and to touch each other's soul

RING-CIRCLES - *Time and Infinity*

Once again, we see here the wheel of life with detailed motifs. The symbolism of the ring is apparent: it deals with eternity, which has neither beginning nor end. The left-hand image with its interwoven bands emphasizes this purpose and illustrates the four distinct points on the compass. The points signify the ultimate infinite nature of the world we experience. The right-hand image is a smooth circle, decorated with interwoven figures signifying totality and unity with all being.

Helps as a talisman to:
- take time for oneself
- find a connection to one's soul
- free oneself

Protects as an amulet against:
- evil spirits and demons
- intrigues

CELTIC CROSSES - *Courage and Trust*

The Celtic Crosses are the link between Celtic and Christian faith. The typical Celtic crosses are on the right and in the middle: a Christian cross, which is encircled by the symbol for the sun. The Celts depicted thus the connection between their old religion and the new. The circle of the sun stands for health, virtue, and security; the cross stands for the presence of the guardian angel. The left-hand cross is very much in the ancient Celtic tradition. Its arms are of equal length and it bears a labyrinthine pattern, which converges, on the center, signifying a harmony between the individual and the universe. The cross is also an intersection, the place of magical meetings. Celtic shamans wore this amulet in order to be in touch with the secret other world and to travel unhindered between the two realms.

Helps as a talisman to:
- keep robust and healthy
- develop courage and confidence
- move through spiritual spheres

Protects as an amulet against:
- dangers on physical as well as spiritual journeys
- retreat from conflict

HEART WITH CELTIC KNOTS - *Love*

The heart in combination with the interwoven Celtic knots symbolizes the love and affection felt for one another. The lines stand for life's journey and for the connection between lovers (love's bands) despite the many entanglements life presents.

Helps as a talisman to:
- attract love
- become romantically attached to another person
- overcome all difficulties together

SHEIAH DOG - *Protection*

Dogs were important companions for the Celts. The Sheiah dog was a guardian of the secrets of the ancient druids and magicians. He moves forward but is looking back, showing that the secrets of the past belong to the future development of mankind.

Helps as a talisman
- in the development and growth of the whole personality
- trace and unlock ancient secrets

Protects as a talisman
- danger in general

Runes

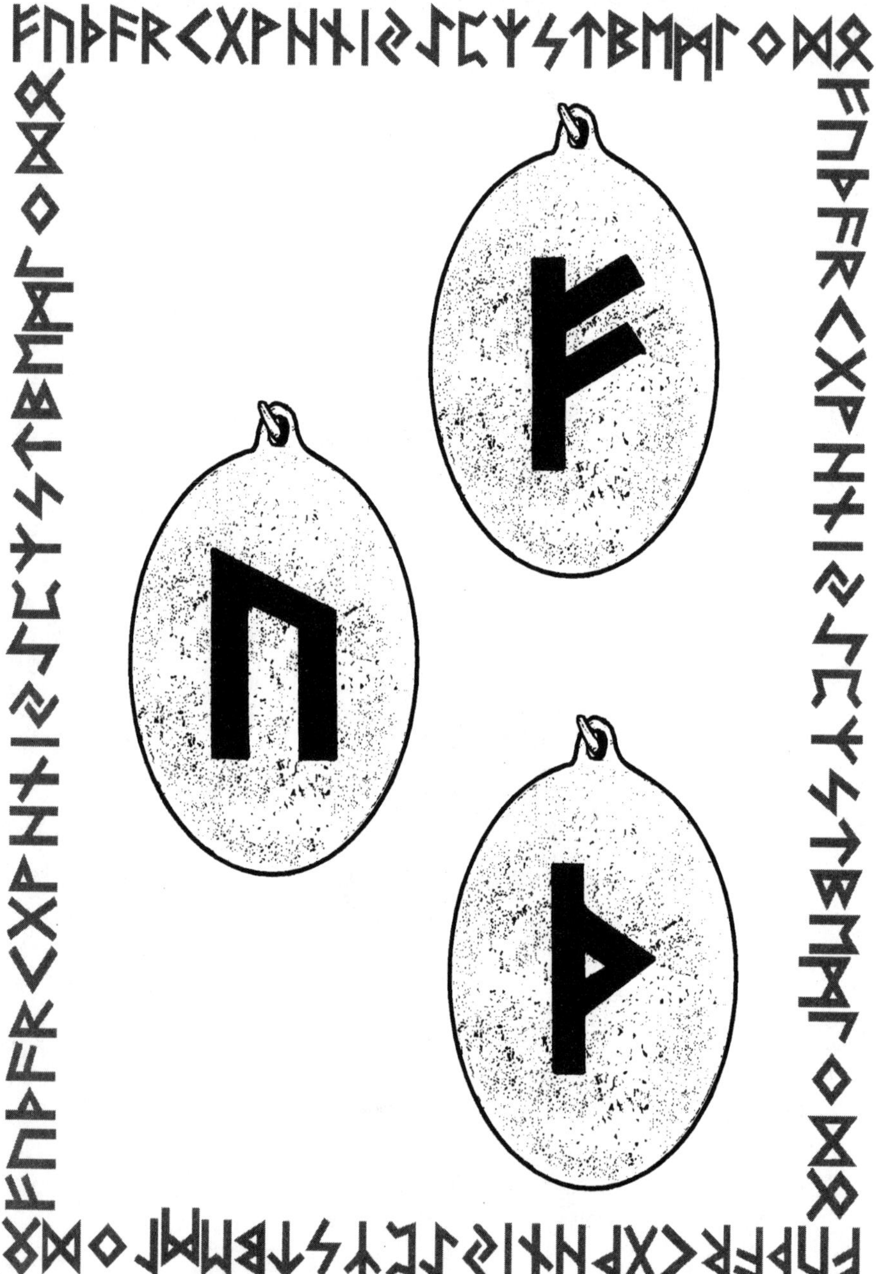

FEHU - *Livestock - Possession*

This rune portrays the horns of cattle. It binds us with possessions and material goods in a secular as well as a divine sense. Thus the two branches reaching toward the sky can also signify arms.

Helps as a talisman to:
- strengthen the physical powers and fertility - unfold all types of fire, everything from campfires to flames of passion - attract riches but only if the rune is called on in moderation

Protects as an amulet against:
- poverty - impotence - powerlessness

URUZ - *Aurochs - Power*

This second rune also represents a cow, in particular, an ox. It tells us how important livestock were to our ancestors. This animal, the Aurochs, is the wild, untamed side of power. When it runs, the earth quakes; to kill such an animal is to have enough to eat throughout the winter.

Helps as a talisman to:
- bring good physical, spiritual, and mental health, for all - bring about lucky circumstances - recognize the context and draw wisdom therefrom

Protects as an amulet against:
- starvation, both physical as well as spiritual - being ubable to ground oneself - anemia

THURISAZ - *Thorn - Patience*

The thorn on a branch serves to fend of evil intentions. The rune also depicts thunder and lightning. It is aligned with Thor's Hammer, the defender of mankind. It is a thorn in the side that drives us onward. It is powers at work beyond our sphere of influence; we can only wait and act deliberately.

Helps as a talisman to:
- wake up and face an attack with colors flying - defend oneself and send opponents into flight - rejuvenate lovers' relations

Protects as an amulet against:
- cowardice - postponing important discussions - repression

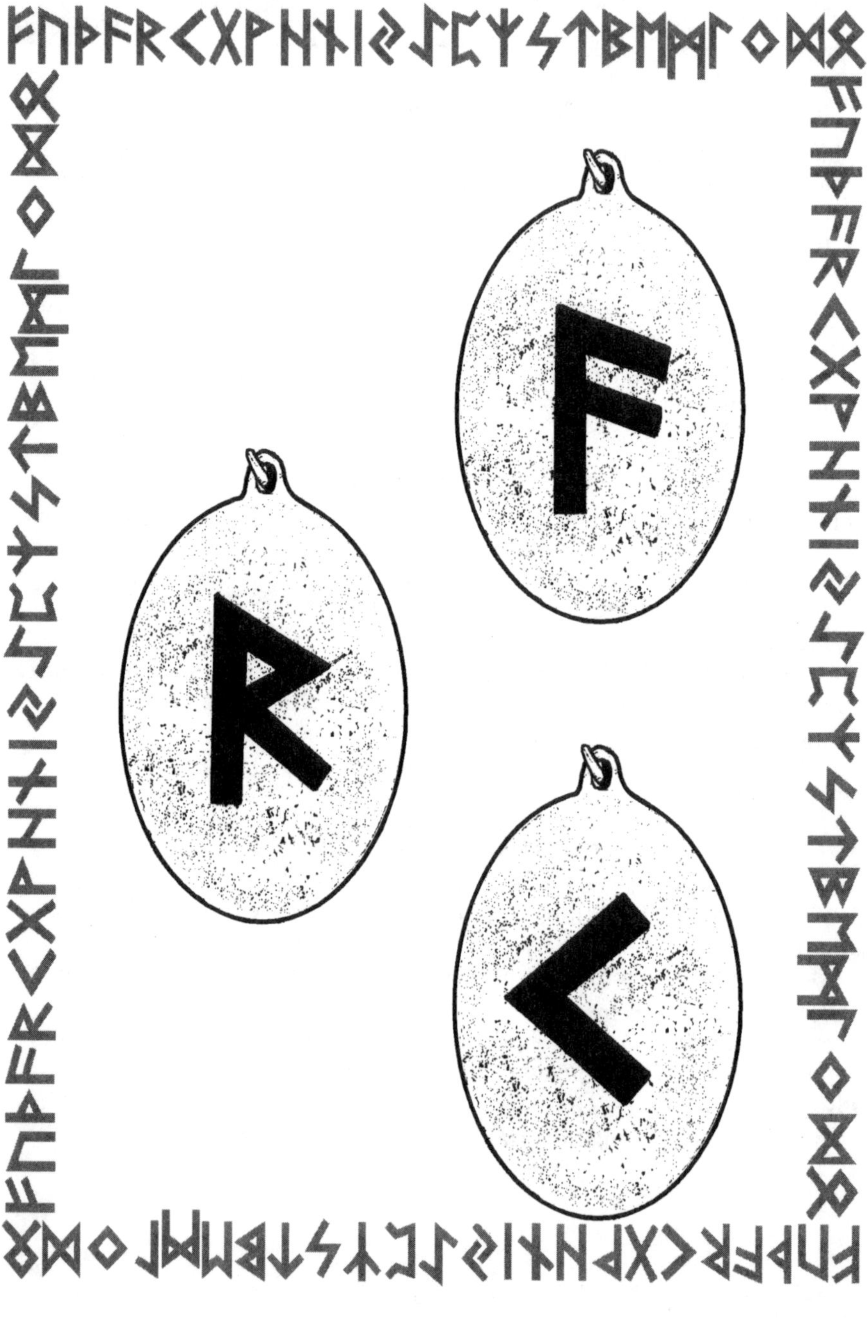

ANSUZ - *God (Ase) - Exchange*

The two crooked lines of the Ansuz rune are like two outstretched arms reaching for another person. They express the desire for spiritual exchange and empathy. This rune endows its wearer with power over language and the ability to infuse words with divine power.

Helps as a talisman to:
- liberate oneself from the chains of fear
- increase magic and clairvoyant abilities
- develop the powers of persuasion

Protects as an amulet against:
- death and fear - being separated from divine knowledge - intrigues and slander

RAIDHO - *Wagon - Union*

The rune displays a straight path and a crooked one. It doesn't matter which path we choose, because, in the end, we'll arrive at the same place. Thus, the rune is thus also associated with movement. It depicts the play between heaven and earth, between the self and the other.

Helps as a talisman to:
- gain access to the "inner way"
- listen to the personal rhythm and to follow it
- with legal proceedings and trials

Protects as an amulet against:
- dangers on travels - chaos - injustice

KENAZ - *The Torch - Opening*

This rune opens itself like a chimney. Its fire burns to get out but it is controlled. The name Kenaz is associated with "kin," that is, the pine torch used to raise a fire so that it illuminates and warms.

Helps as a talisman to:
- transform and renew oneself
- control one's energies
- increase one's love of life

Protects as an amulet against:
- undesirable influences- fire- inflammations and infections

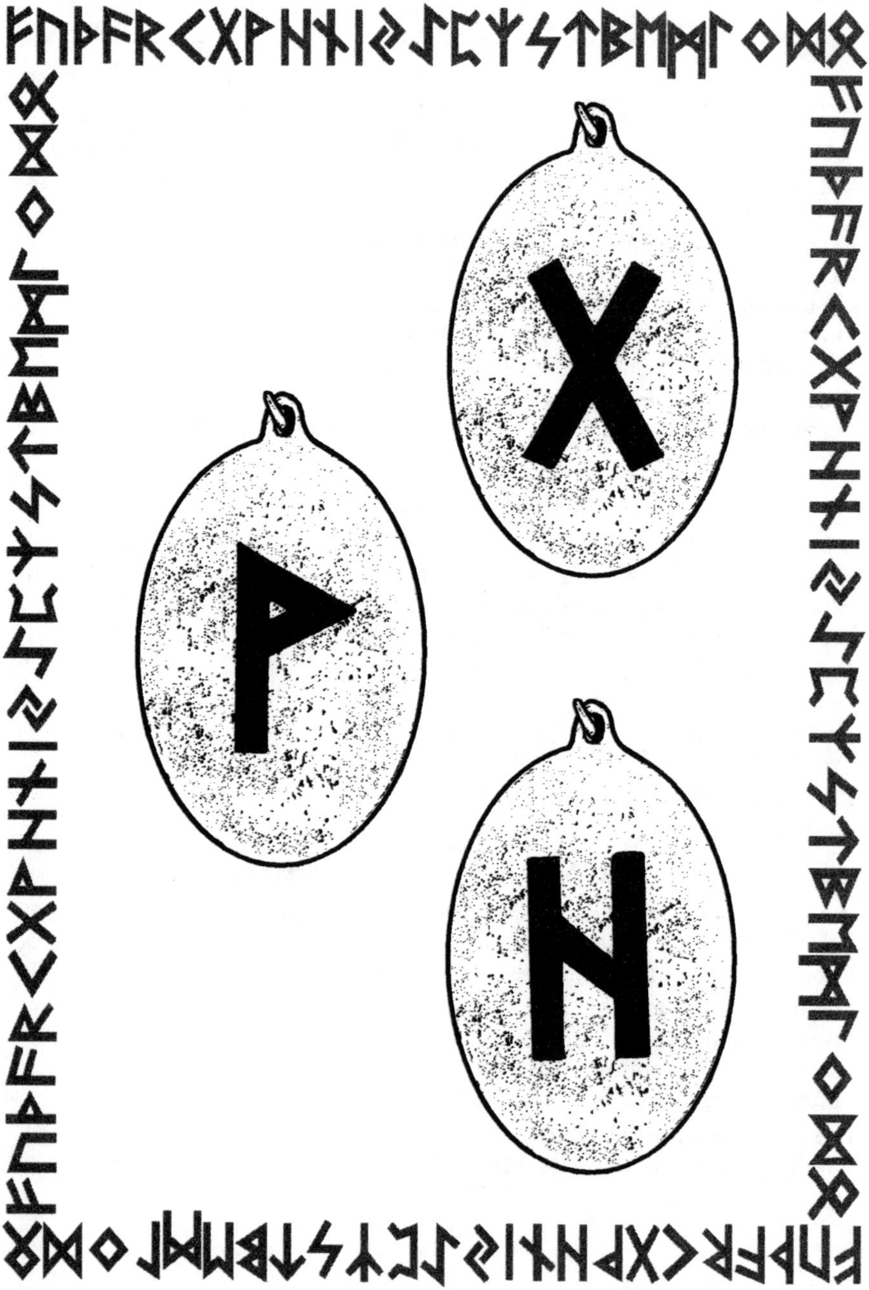

GEBO - *The Gift - Partnership*

Two hatched lines portray the interwoven nature of two individual units. Each gives to the other. Giving creates a new whole. We can also perceive in the rune, the meeting of two corners, which converge and exchange with each other.

Helps as a talisman to:
- be generous
- receive a gift of god
- attain unity in love

Protects as an amulet against:
- stinginess - conflict between siblings and lovers - the ingratitude and indignity of a gift

WUNJO - *Happiness - Joy*

This rune looks like a pennant or clan flag. It points to a feeling of belonging together or kinship, even if the members of a group are different. Happiness is, however, to be found in the feeling of being able to rely on the others.

Helps as a talisman to:
- feel comfortable as a part of a team
- experience happiness and well-being
- be able to rely on one's friends

HAGAL - *Hail - Elementary Violence*

The rune stands in the ninth position, which is the most holy and secret of all runes: the number of fulfillment, which leads to the extension of power and of talents. The turn within has the effect of producing a stronger turn to the outside. The two vertical lines are separated by a bar and thus kept in balance.

Helps as a talisman to:
- actively defend oneself
- close rooms and to protect them
- reestablish harmony

Protects as an amulet against:
- attacks and misfortunes - devastation through bad weather conditions - everything (this is the protective rune!)

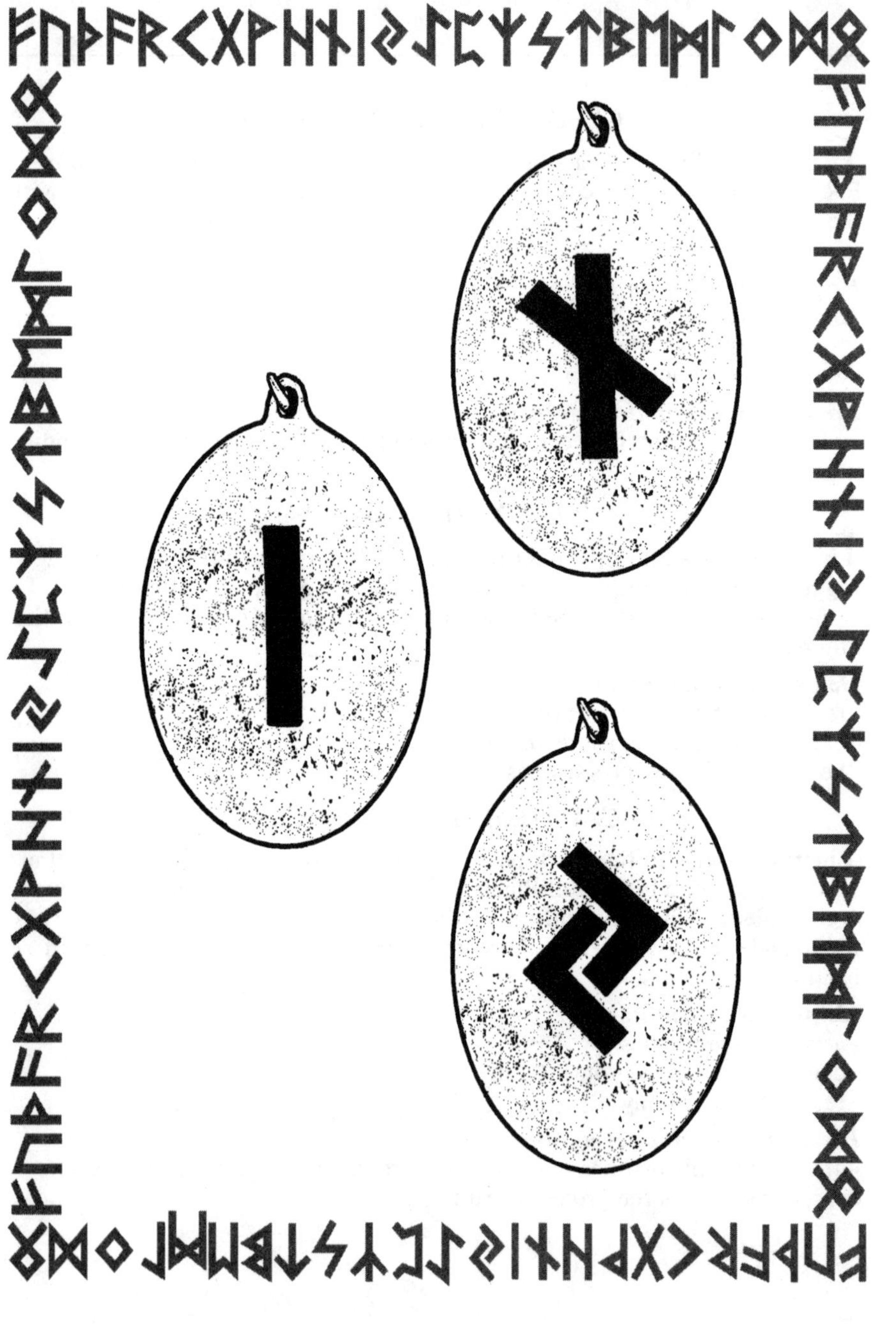

NAUDIZ - *Need - Pain*

This is a man in need. Something has crossed him. Change is n
alter fate. We do not have to suffer passively but can intervene in our own
fate. We can light a fire with two sticks and thus diminish our need.

Helps as a talisman to:
- overcome suffering
- enhance creativity
- eliminate stress and hate

Protects as an amulet against:
- depression - inconsolability - dependence

ISA - *Ice - Standstill*

The rune depicts the steadfast individual, who can be frozen in routine but
also independent. This is the Roman numeral "one," the individual, and the
English "I." It represents a concentrated force of will. It is the axis that
binds sky, earth, and the underworld.

Helps as a talisman to:
- bring something to a standstill, to meditate
- develop telepathic powers and break through the cosmic levels with
shamanic powers
- keep to a straight path

Protects as an amulet against:
- crippling influences - outer and inner unrest - undesirable forces

JERA - *Year - Harvest*

The sky and the earth are brought together in a holy mill, which prepares
the seed that will after a time of becoming make the harvest possible. The
twelfth rune embodies the twelve-fold yearly course of the sun. The two figures on the rune symbolize giving and taking, the fair exchange and the
reward.

Helps as a talisman to:
- have a good harvest and to make undertakings successful
- see the circle of life and to enter into its flow
- bring about peace and harmony

Protects as an amulet against:
- chronic tardiness - infertility - poor harvests or failures

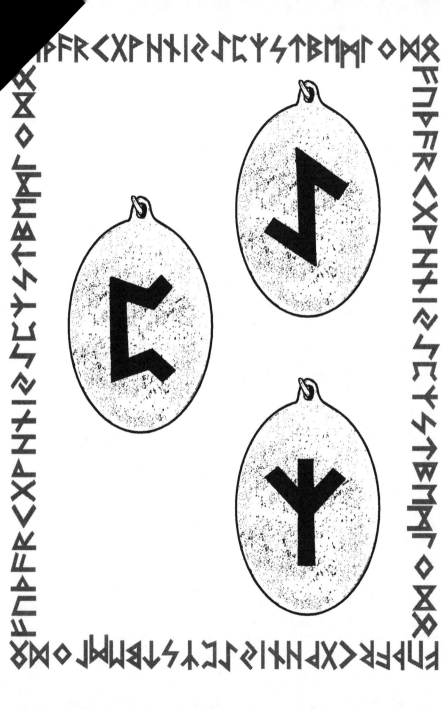

EIWAZ - *Yew Tree - Defense*

The upright yew gives us its shadow where we can move through another level of reality. Its deep roots allow it to survive the many centuries. We can learn endurance and far-sightedness, strength and flexibility. The wood of the yew tree is hard, but at the same time flexible enough to be used for a bow. This brings it into contact with death, which also brings mankind life, because the hunted and slain animal nourishes.

Helps as a talisman to:
- be at peace with the world beyond - become aware of one's own family tree - increase endurance and will power

Protects as an amulet against:
- the fear of death - deception, betrayal, and delusion - undesirable, destructive influences

PERTHROM- *Dice Cup - Initiation*

A cup rolls on its side and the dice spill out, determining our fate and fortune. The oracle tells us about our past, present, and future. It helps us to become familiar with the flow of time and law of cause and effect.

Helps as a talisman to:
- know your predestination - discover the best time for an undertaking - be lucky in gambling

Protects as an amulet against:
- losses from gambling - irresponsibility - birth problems

ALGIZ - *Elk - Protection*

This rune depicts the antlers of the elk, which serve to protect and defend not only him but also its family. The raven's foot is also apparent here, and this makes it a bridge between the different worlds.

Helps as a talisman to:
- defend and protect - make oneself understood to spirits - enhance vitality

Protects as an amulet against:
- weakening of the immune system - dangers in the struggle for life - fear of the unknown

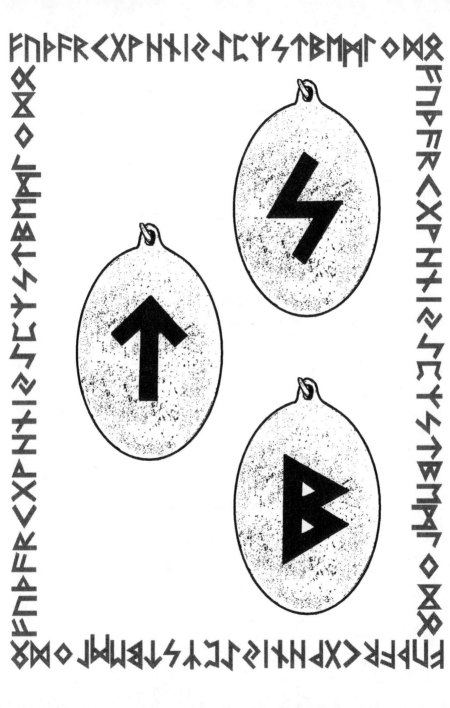

SOWILO - *The Sun - Sun Wheel*

This rune looks like a ray of light. A part of the wheel of the sun, constantly turning, is depicted here. The gliding power of the sun travels down to earth and gives us its energy so that we can live in ecstasy.

Helps as a talisman to:
- awaken the chakras - enhance the higher will and vitality - be successful - make a profit - come away in victory

Protects as an amulet against:
- blocked energy - being prudish - inner darkness

TIWAZ - *Gott Tyr - Justice*

Like an arrow pointing upward, the rune strikes the target only if it has been well aimed and is pointed straight. We should lead our lives in the same way, not hesitating but heading straight for our goal. The rune is also a protective rune for all types of needs: the name of the god is Tyr, which is French "tirer," to shoot.

Helps as a talisman to:
- create spiritual order and develop the power of faith
- successfully conclude legal proceedings
- sacrifice oneself for the success of the group

Protects as an amulet against:
- bending the law - unscrupulous ambition - waiting too long and hesitation

BERKANA - *Beech - Growth*

The rune portrays the mother's breasts. Naturally, it also recalls the letter "B." The newborn feels safe and secure at the mother's breast. Berkana means beech and cradles were made of beech wood. This rune stands in the eighteenth position, pointing to the great secret of birth and rebirth.

Helps as a talisman to:
- have feelings of safety and security
- let everything gradually grow
- set off the creative process

Protects as an amulet against:
- accidents
- difficult births
- suffering for being a woman and against repressed femininity

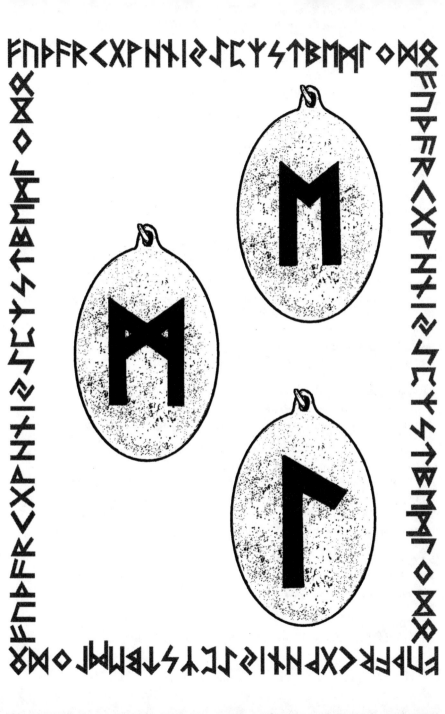

EHWAZ - *Horse - Movement*

The rune could signify two people reaching out their hands for each other; it could also be a horse. Sometimes the rune is even interpreted as two horses side-by-side, because in the Germanic tradition the structure of power is expressed through two horses.

Helps as a talisman to:
- further collaboration
- undertake journeys through the here and beyond
- ensure fidelity and dependability

Protects as an amulet against:
- being alone - power struggles - renunciation of the world beyond

MANNAZ - *Man - The Self*

This shows two people entering into a close relationship. It can also be interpreted as someone with divine inclinations. The complete person is depicted here; he or she unites the male and the female.

Helps as a talisman to:
- be more humane
-clarify one's thoughts
- unite in love

Protects as an amulet against:
- one-dimensional perception of oneself - being separated from divine connection - inhumanity and the pleasure in other's suffering

LAGUZ - *Water, Leek - Flow*

The leek rises from the ground and tells us of the magic of herbs. The leek was the German-Celtic equivalent of the Roman laurel, the prize for the young warrior after victory in battle. The rune can also be understood as a fountain, the secret source of all life.

Helps as a talisman to:
- enhance fertility and vitality
- withstand difficult tests
- travel safe and secure

Protects as an amulet against:
- accidents and poisoning - cowardice and betrayal - calcification - emergencies on water

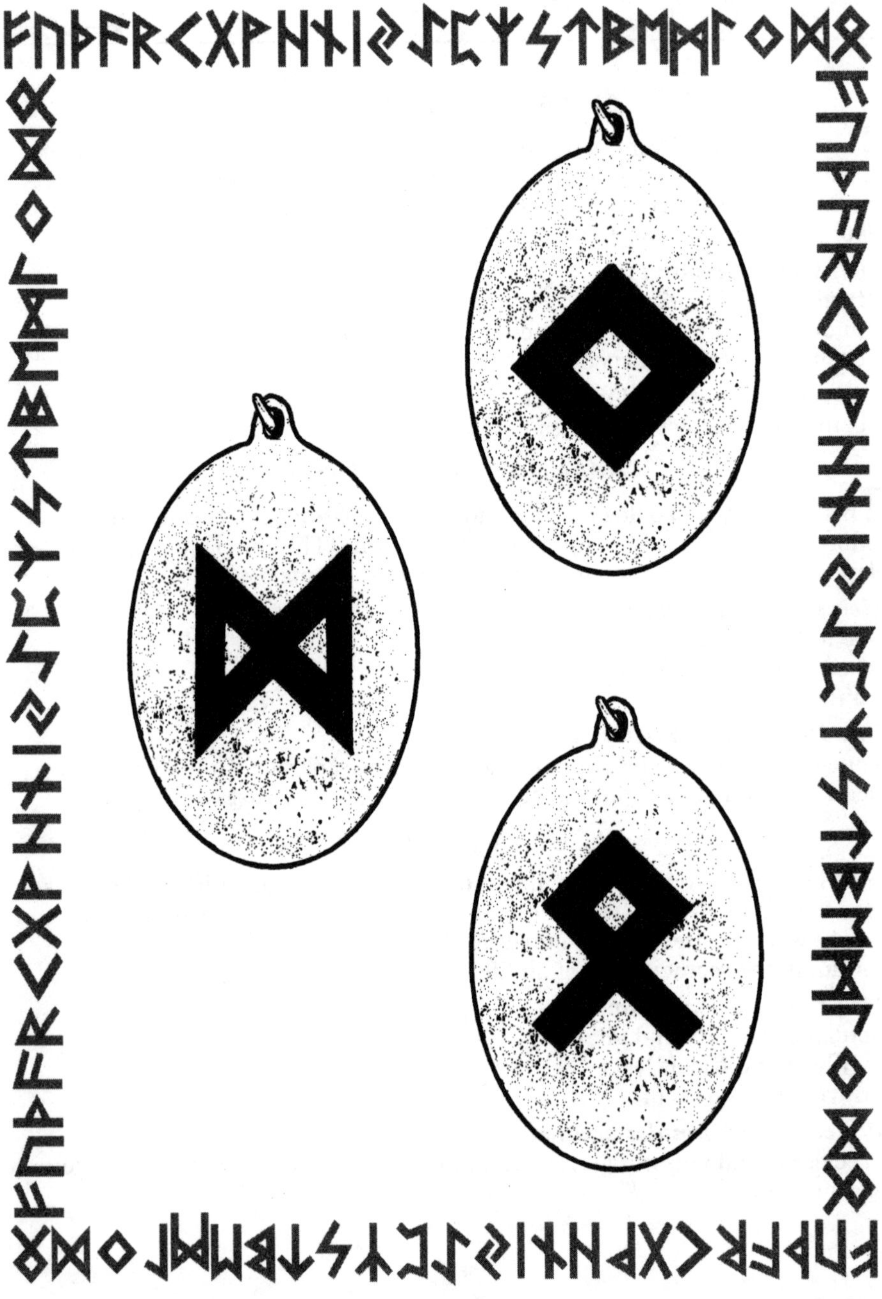

INGWAZ - *Ing the God-Hero - The Egg*

The four walls of the rune enclose a protected space, where something can grow and ripen, like an egg after fertilization. The egg nourishes and provides energy, which is withheld in order to burst forth in the spring with incredible energy. Think of the Easter egg!

Helps as a talisman to:
- unfold new powers in peace and quiet
- during pregnancy
- suddenly release energies; to break through the shell

Protects as an amulet against:
- destructive attacks - the loss of power - heavy, counterproductive activity

DAGAZ - *The Day - Dawn*

A new day dawns. Light cuts through the darkness. Perhaps Venus is the morning star in the sky. In the mystical moment, our dreams and ideals become clear, something "dawns" on us.

Helps as a talisman to:
- pierce the gray areas
- perceive one's surroundings and their influence
- increase persistence and endurance, when attaining an important goal

Protects as an amulet against:
- narrow-mindedness - indiscretion - unproductive environmental conditions

OTHALA - *Home - The Legacy*

This rune portrays the protected space (see INGWAZ) in a state of mutual exchange with its surroundings. The egg has been broken open, and the fledgling can get to know the world around it from the protection of its home. Material well-being can also be improved by setting this boundary.

Helps as a talisman to:
- find one's true home
- establish one's inheritance and to pass on one's legacy
- attain human freedom within legal society
- multiply wealth and well-being

Protects as an amulet against:
- egoistic thought and deed - loss of roots - the feeling of not being at home anyplace

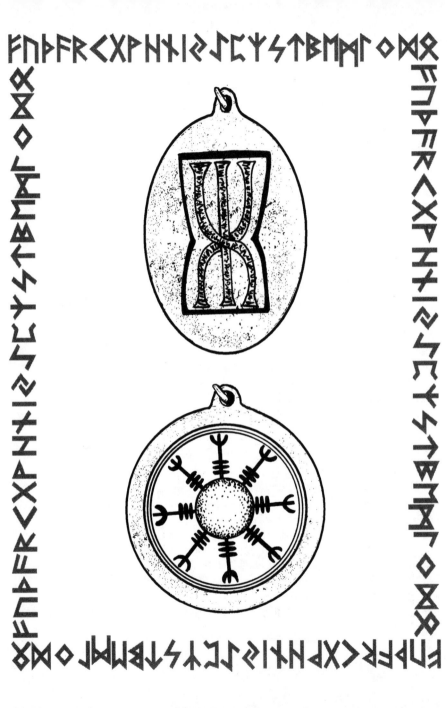

THOR'S SCEPTER - *Property and Profit Rune of Well-Being*

The Vikings not only used the rune alphabet but also attributed magical powers to a number of symbols. The one in the illustration depicts the scepter of the powerful god of thunder, Thor. The three interwoven bolts of lightning represent the twists and turns of fate. This rune is a powerful protective amulet, especially well-suited to ward off theft and other misfortunes.

Helps as a talisman to:
- ensure well-being
- defend one's property

Protects as an amulet against:
- jealousy and envy of others
- robbery and environmental disasters

RUNE OF IRRESISTIBILITY - *Attraction and Victory*

Eight spokes emanate from the hub of a wheel, which represents a protective rune. The spokes end in elk antlers, which recall the Algiz rune. The three lines through each spoke, twenty-four in total, signify the protective powers of the rune circle. This amulet protects its wearer, while at the same time sending out rays of overwhelming power into the world. Chiefs and heads of clans wore this rune to instill their will upon others.

Helps as a talisman to:
- be irresistible in love, war, and business
- develop powerful charisma

Protects as an amulet against:
- subjugation
- a shadow life

The Middle Ages

THE GREEN MAN - *Nature Protector*

The green man is ancient Europe's protector of nature. He is an ancient symbol for our connection to the earth. The green man is also known as Cernunnos (Celtic). His face is often found on the facade of medieval churches, where he is a protective spirit. He is equated with the oak and one of his forerunners is the Greek god Pan, the goat-footed god.

Helps as a talisman to:
- protect nature and the environment
- reconcile oneself with nature
- observe animals in the wild

Protects as an amulet against:
- losing one's way outdoors
- wild animals

THE SWORD OF DAVID - *Justice*

The sword has been a powerful amulet since the time of King David, both as real sword and as symbol. The sword symbolizes the battle for justice against ignorance. The just person looks at both sides of a matter before deciding. This accords him, of course, honor and authority.

Helps as a talisman to:
- practice fairness and not be cheated
- stand up for something with authority and valor

Protects as an amulet against:
- all types of anxieties and sufferings
- clear enemies and conspiracies
- injustice

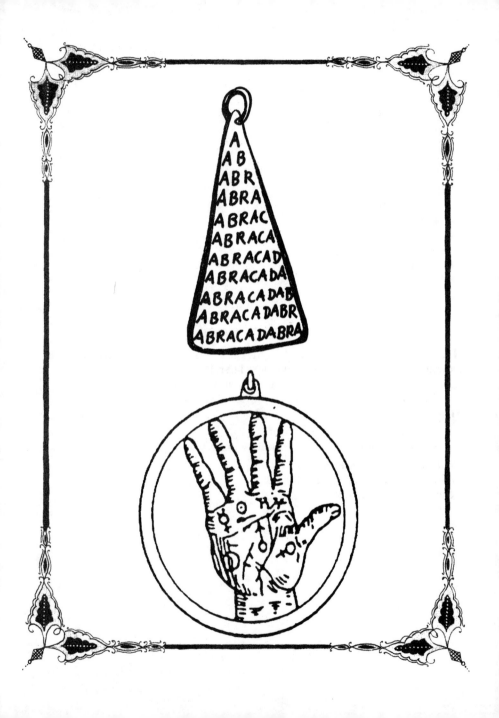

ABRACADABRA - *Unexpected Good Fortune*

This is one of the most famous amulets in history. Abracadabra is mentioned for the first time in the 3rd century in the liber medicinalis of Quintus Serenus Sammonicus, verse 935, where one finds the equation of the Celtic abra (god) and cad (holy). In the Middle Ages, it was used as a magical word. The eleven letters like the eleven rows point to divine law. The disappearing schema of the word on the amulet empowers the charm. The loss of a letter with each new row and the final "a" represents the translation of god's law to earth. "A" is the original syllable and thus the breath of god that blows through us.

Helps as a talisman to:
- acquire magical powers
- attract unexpected luck
- eliminate illness through the disappearing schema of letters

Protects as an amulet against:
- injustice and evil events

THE LUCKY HAND - *Joy*

The lucky hand has many uses. This amulet shows the zodiac according to the lines of the hand. In ancient Babylon, the right hand was associated with the goddess Venus. The outstretched hand has been depicted in natural as well as stylized form since the ancient Egyptians. It was widespread in late antiquity and in the Middle Ages. Its wearer should always have good fortune in his hands or through work done with the hands. We can also recognize a natural gesture of defense against physical attack in the upraised hand. The amulet protects against spiritual attacks as well.

Helps as a talisman to:
- open the window of opportunity
- bring joy and happiness

Protects as an amulet against:
- occult attacks and ill-will of all types

THE TREE OF LIFE - *Growth*

In many cultures, the tree of life is a common symbol. The tree unites heaven and earth. In all human communities, the tree has a special place. Druids, Babylonians, Hebrews, Norwegians, Greeks, Chinese, and many others tell myths of the "tree of life." It is a symbol of growth, healing, and old age. Trees represent the magic qualities of nature.

Helps as a talisman to:
- fulfill one's inner and outer growth with power
- be healed through binding oneself to the power of the tree
- reach a ripe old age

Protects as an amulet against:
- the loss of one's roots
- growth disorders

THE COSMIC EGG - *Infinity*

The symbol of the cosmic egg expresses the creation of the universe from the great void. It was a symbol in ancient cultures. The egg in the illustration consists of Arabic figures, which means that all things are contained in creation. In the beginning, all things were one. Out of this one, arose the many.

Helps as a talisman to:
- see creation as a whole
- recognize the whole in creation's parts
- observe each part of creation as complete in itself
- learn about everything in creation through one part
- know the infinite truth
- develop modesty and humility

The eight magic talismans that follow come originally from Poland. The symbols were found on the magic belt of a knight, which can be seen today in the Warsaw Museum. Such signs were worn by medieval knights around the throat, waist, or on parts of their armor. The effect of each individual talisman is described below.

DETERMINATION

Eight spokes around a hub. The number eight signifies the infinity and the faith in god. Two of the spokes end in points, which are aimed upward. The spokes are powerful. This stability carries over to the bearer of the sign. The points on the ends of spokes combat insecurity.

Helps as a talisman to:
- alleviate insecurity
- attack one's goals with determination
- overcome spiritual frailties

DESTINY

This symbol shows a cross that points in all four compass directions. Another cross, the cross of Christ, appears at its apex. The horizontal lines bear roots on the left and a tree crown on the right; it symbolizes the surface of the earth. On the horizontal axis there is also an imperial orb, which symbolizes the union of divine and secular. In the lower left quadrant, there is a horseshoe, symbol of permanence.

Helps as a talisman to:
- develop ambition
- bring god and man to act quickly
- know one's destiny and to follow it with determination

HEALTH

This signet shows that the knights who wore it took part in the crusades. The circle is divided by a cross into four quadrants and bears a quartered circle in the center, in which the letters ARAF stand. Araf is the bonfire of Islam, which is supposed to lie beneath the cliffs of the Omar mosque in Jerusalem. The souls enter this fire and wait for the final judgment. On the left, there are knights who stand outside the bonfire. On the right, the sign for Saturn, a snake, tells us that the knights are beyond sin. In the upper portion of the talisman, there is the upper half of a cross, which signifies this earth. The upper branch of the great nature cross bends into a tendril, signifying life.

Helps as a talisman to:
- maintain good health
- preserve one's vitality
- increase one's self-consciousness

ADDICTION

This amulet depicts, once again, eight spokes, a reference to the infinite nature of god's power. The horizontal line is crossed by three lines, which represent the threefold nature of the exchange between inner and outer worlds. On the right, we have the same symbol for the world, however, with the symbol "TR," which indicates the word Trisagion (threefold holy). The letters "A" and "M" mean Anno and Mundi, which here refers to the beginning of the world. As a whole the signet conveys the threefold unity of god the father, son, and Holy Spirit.

Protects as an amulet against:
- bad habits
- spiritual problems and dark moods
- addictions of all sorts

LOVE

In the illustration, we see a quadrant in the center that stands on edge and is divided by a cross. This symbolizes the Word of God. The names of the four evangelists are written around the edges, representing the strengthening of the Word of God in our world.

Helps as a talisman to:
- win the heart of a beloved
- bear God's love within oneself

SECURITY

The encircled triangle with the point aimed upward describes the spiritual striving for God. In each of the three corners there is: an "A" (on its head), an "M" meaning Anno Mundi, which means "since the beginning of the world"; the arrow stands for the ambition that touches the inner heart of man. God will bless all work done by the wearer of this pendant.

Helps as a talisman to:
- succeed at work
- be certain in the knowledge that one's work stands under the blessing of God

EMOTIONS

Before a battle or tournament, the knight wrapped his sword with the colors of his beloved: she enveloped him. In the illustration, this band frames the letters belonging to this knight. He cannot escape his bond of love. The lady still waits outside, but she is certain of her power over her knight. If he is victorious, she belongs to him.

Helps as a talisman to:
- be forthright in one's feelings
- lead to a happy love
- lead to lasting friendship

Protects as an amulet against:
- infidelity
- inconsistency
- doubting the beloved

RELATIONS

The Pentagram is a symbol for love. It is borne by a cross, which proclaims hope and the calling of God. The letter "I" and "G" stand for IEHOVA (Greek) and GOD (English). The signet is a symbol for the assurance of God that love will remain true.

Helps as a talisman to:
- keep the beloved person, be that person a lover, partner, or friend
- develop qualities that please the beloved person
- trust in God

WELL-BEING

A sword symbolizing the knight pierces an "S" in the middle of the amulet. The "S" stands for the sun, which is the center of our lives and is also the center of mankind. Above this, there is an oval, which portrays the visible heavens. The crown over it stands for God, who watches over all. The crosses on the right and left are temporal crosses, which represent in this case the visible and invisible world and reflect the four directions of the heavens.

Helps as a talisman to:
- find power, strength, and force
- live well in wealth and from God's mercy
- bring in a good harvest and profit from the excess

GENERAL PROTECTION

Dr. John Dee (1527-1608) was a famous mathematician and astrologist. His intellectual activities touch on broad fields of the occult. He was, amongst other things, an advisor to Queen Elizabeth I and an alchemist at the court of King Rudolf II in Prague, who also supported Kepler. He proposed the Henochioc system. In Gustav Meyrink's novel "The Angel from the Western Window," Dee's life and work are described in detail. His writings comprise 78 volumes, which refers to the numerology of the tarot. On his most famous table, magic quadrants are engraved that provide a powerful form of protection. Seven small quadrants frame a moderately larger one. Seven is the number that links heaven and earth, but it also refers to the Big Dipper, which represented the great mother in pre-Christian times. The eighth quadrant in the middle represents the link to royal power, which arises from the infinite.

Helps as a talisman to:
- acquire strength and power through the divine

Protects as an amulet against:
- dangers and forces from the visible as well as invisible world

PENTAGRAM - *Wish Fulfillment*

The Pentagram is also known as the druid's foot. It is drawn either as an invocation (beginning at the upper corner and ending at the lower left) or a protective ritual (beginning lower left and ending upper corner). This ritual is used to develop the magical capacities of the human personality. The Pentagram existed as a symbol in ancient times. For Pythagoras, it was a sign of health. In the Middle Ages, it was used in magic formulas to gain power over elemental forces. The Pentagram acquired the appellation "druid's foot," because it was thought to protect against witches and druids. Today it is the symbol of the microcosm. The illustration shows the light-Pentagram. As a star it provides access to secret powers that we can use to reach our goals.

Helps as a talisman to:
- fulfill wishes
- invoke spiritual powers and to retain them in order to raise the personality to a higher level
- activate inner powers in order to attain outer goals

Protects as an amulet against:
- witchcraft
- the "evil eye" by casting the evil back upon its cause

HEPTAGRAM - *Mysterious Star*

This symbol is sacred to Venus, the goddess of love. In ancient astrology there are seven planets; we know seven basic sounds, seven colors, seven beams, seven weekdays, etc. On the cabalistic tree of life, the seventh Sephirah represents that of Venus. Because the number seven consists of the divine three and the secular four, the Heptagram refers to the whole person: the physical body and the divine soul.

Helps as a talisman to:
- attain harmony and love
- radiate beauty and attractiveness

THE ROSE PENTACLE - *Secrecy*

This fivefold symbol represents unlimited existence, immortality. The rose is the gateway to secrets and stands for secrecy. The Pentagram symbolizes the four elements and the principle of spirit (upper point). Whoever lives in full consciousness and has discovered the secret behind creation is silent.

Helps as a talisman to:
- be rejuvenated
- strengthen the aura
- know one's immortal soul
- be silent about one's knowledge

Protects as an amulet against:
- the urge to proselytize
- doubt
- animosity

HEXAGRAM - *Knowledge*

Seal of Soloman or David's Star
This star is perhaps the best known. It consists of two triangles. The one pointing upward symbolizes the spiritual. The other pointing down embodies the physical. The hexagram in the middle is the Sephirah of the sun on the cabalistic tree of life; it is associated with the heart in relationships. King Solomon used this symbol as a signet to invoke demons that built his temple in Jerusalem. Then he used it to dispel them. The star enhances good moods and gives inner peace and self-confidence.

Helps as a talisman to:
- attain harmony and balance
- gain insight and knowledge
- study magic and invoke angels

Protects as an amulet against:
- the power of evil
- illness, misfortune, and mishap

SUN COIN - *Health*

This talisman was originally made of gold, the metal of the sun. Around the border, one can read that it was prepared with the seven minerals. Each of the seven corresponds to the planets grouped around the sun. The sun stands for the divine light of the individual spirit. The planets complete the sun so that the talisman represents a holistic means of healing.

Helps as a talisman to:
- find health, well-being, and happiness
- evoke the powers of the planets in one's cause

AGRIPPA'S PENTAGRAM - *Man*

The number five stands for man. We have five fingers on each hand and five toes on each foot; man also has five senses. Agrippa von Nettesheim (1486-1535) successfully overturned many prejudices of his age and proposed a system of cabalistic philosophy. The adjoining Pentagram depicting man with arms and legs outspread illustrates how he forms a Pentagram. The arms and legs represent the four elements, the main principle of spirit. The five planets (Mercury, Venus, Mars, Jupiter, and Saturn) stand at these extruding body parts. Sun and moon stand directly on the body: the sun on the solar plexus, the center of man, and the moon at the sexual organs, which represents the unconscious.

Helps as a talisman to:
- conquer the heart of the beloved
- attain insight through prayer and come closer to god

Protects as an amulet against:
- visible and invisible evil forces

SUN TALISMAN - *Fame*

In the illustration of one of Solomon's seals, we find twelve names of God in twelve fields as a tetragramaton in Hebrew letters. Yood Hey Vauv Hey. Christians know this name from the New Testament: Jehovah. The twelve fields indicate the twelve months of the year, that is, at the course of the sun. With this talisman we ask for help our life long.

Helps as a talisman to:
- develop power, joy of life, self-confidence, and a clear spirit
- develop social and private friendships
- have successes for oneself
- begin a new undertaking under fortuitous circumstances
- become famous

MOON TALISMAN - *Artistic Success*

This form of the moon house is very ancient. According to descriptions it can be traced to the signet of King Solomon some 3,000 years ago. Jehovah is called upon here, under his name and various other names. The moon pendent affects the independent side of human life like poetry, art, music, and spirituality.

Protects as a talisman to:
- discover one's artistic talents and develop them
- recognize and promote one's communicative capabilities
- overcome obstacles

MERCURY TALISMAN - *Intelligence*

This pendant is also attributed to King Solomon. The inner circle with the twelve-point star was actually designed by Solomon; the outer circle is, however, a Latin phrase from the Middle Ages: Wisdom and strength live in his house and the knowledge of all things resides with him from eternity to eternity. Within the star, Hebrew letters have been inserted, each of which has meaning as an incantation. We see, too, the tetragram: Yood Hey Vav Hey. In the middle are the letters "AL" which also stand for god. This talisman enables god to take over the mercurial capacities: intellect and the ability to learn.

Helps as a talisman to:
- better concentrate
- increase the brain's capacity for learning

Protects as an amulet against:
- idiocy
- ignorance

VENUS TALISMAN - *Love*

Two triangles meet like two people. The many names of god are engraved in Hebrew, among these are Yood Hey Vav Hey and Adonai. This, too, is a seal of King Solomon's; it can be used by its wearer to invoke the power of Venus.

Helps as a talisman to:
- receive the love of the desired person
- enhance one's own attractive powers
- build new friendships
- harmonize existing relations
- show one's feelings by giving the talisman

MARS TALISMAN - *Defense and Healing*

The Mars talisman contains the hexagram, which reveals the connection to the positive side of man, since the hexagram is associated with the sun. In addition, it is a seal of Solomon and therefore has a protective power. In the center one sees different names for god in Hebrew letters. In the six corners there stand a "Hey," which symbolizes the word "five." The fifth Sephirah on the cabalistic tree of life belongs to Mars.

Helps as a talisman to:
- increase the defensive powers of the body
- balance out the active and passive forces in man
- support healing of all sorts
- enhance the performance of medicine

JUPITER TALISMAN - *Luck in Gambling*

This talisman is also a seal of Solomon and consists of a hexagram, a sun symbol. In the middle, a horseshoe catches the good luck. The horse is a symbol for good luck in many cultures and the horseshoe is thus associated with this luck, too. The triangle pointing upward indicates the intent with which one plays. The letter "Pe" in the six fields represents the number 80, and the letter "Qoph" seven times on the border the number 100. The high numbers bring good luck in gambling.

Helps as a talisman to:
- be lucky in gambling
- decide to play or not to play
- maintain one's balance even with losses
- play within one's means

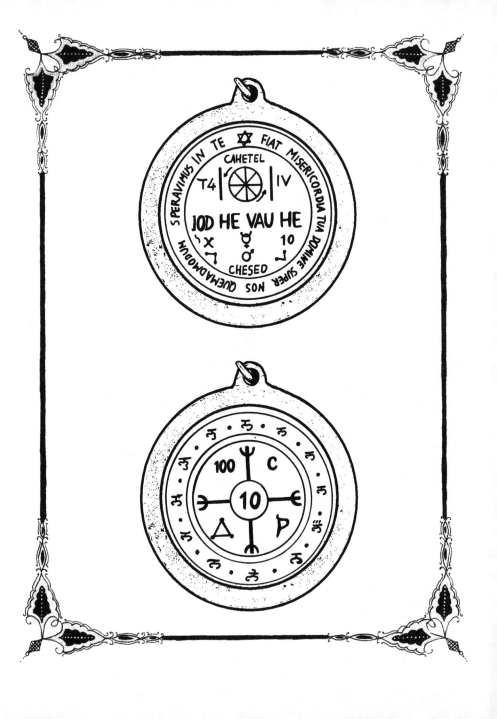

THE MAGIC CIRCLE - *Money*

The outer circle is a Latin invocation that reads: Lord, have mercy on us; we beseech you. In the center of the pendant, one finds the convergence of the four with the ten. The number four stands for Jupiter or god, the father; ten stands for the earth. The wheel with its eight spokes symbolizes the endless turning of the earth. The letter "Daled" is the fourth letter in the Hebrew alphabet. "Chesed" is the fourth Sephirah on the cabalistic tree of life and it is associated with Jupiter. "Caheteel," the angels who live on it, Mercury, the thinker, and Mars, the fighter, close out the circle.

Helps as a talisman to:
- prove intuition in social opportunities
- achieve success in trade and commerce
- make the correct social decisions
- increase one's wealth

CHARM-AMULET - *Casting and Breaking*

This amulet contains symbols from several cultures. The number ten in a circle signifies the Western world. The number 100 is written in Arabic, Latin, Hebrew, and Henochish letters throughout the four quadrants. The rune Algiz protects four times externally. Twelve times OM appears around the border.

Helps as a talisman to:
- remove a spell
- confuse and confound attackers
- sleep well

Protects as an amulet against:
- magic, witchcraft, vampires, and ghosts
- nightmares
- delusions

COUPLE TALISMAN - *Union*

Bet is the number two, which stands, in this case, for the couple. The number ten indicates the earth, where this coupling occurs. The letter Bet appears in the lower left, in Hebrew, in the middle as a magic symbol, and on the lower right in Henochish lettering. Around the border, the Hebrew letter Vav (number 6, the lovers in the tarot) and Bet (number 2, union) appear seven times. Seven is the holy number that unites heaven and earth. The triangles united represent the union of male and female.

Helps as a talisman to:
- create goodwill and harmony between partners
- overcome obstacles in marriage and love relations
- resolve sexual conflicts
- increase sexual potency

TALISMAN OF WEALTH - *Gold*

Various geometric shapes are arranged around a geometric symbol for happiness. The inner circle represents the earth. The rhombus symbolizes stability. The number ten is used in numerous texts in Latin, Hebrew, Henochish, Egyptian, and Arabic. The word "Aurum" (gold) dominates the talisman. Everything is directed toward the growth and multiplication of wealth.

Helps as a talisman to:
- multiply one's wealth
- make financial profits
- improve one's finances
- remember one's spiritual well-being in spite of wealth

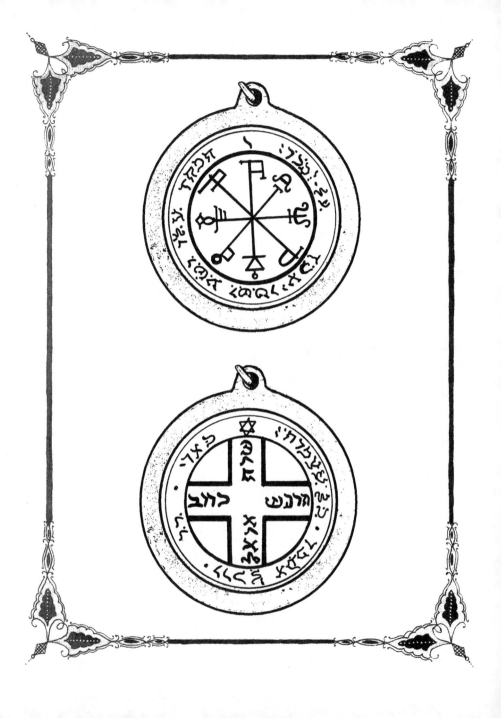

TALISMAN OF THE JOY OF LIFE - *Relaxation*

Eight spokes radiate outwards. They bear alchemists' symbols, which improve the process of transformation. In the outer wheel, the Hebrew names of god are invoked.

Helps as a talisman to:
- fortify one's good humor and happiness
- relax
- meet resistance with ease

Protects as an amulet against:
- fear
- depression
- loneliness

PROTECTIVE AMULET - *Journey*

The adjoining illustration shows the earthly cross as intersection within a circle. The amulet depicts the four compass points with their corresponding protective spirits. The names of god are invoked around the edges.

Helps as a talisman to:
- withstand dangerous tests
- overcome known and unknown opponents
- find lodging on a journey

Protects as an amulet against:
- accidents in the country, in water, in the air, and underground
- misfortune on a journey

UNIVERSAL TALISMAN - *Renewal*

The magic quadrant rules over this amulet, whose design is based on the number five. Five is associated with the planet Mars, which defines health. The numbers alongside the quadrant produce the number fifteen, which stands for nature. Below the quadrant,one finds the seal of Samuel, the angel that corresponds to Mars and governs Tuesday. The astrological signs are around the border.

Helps as a talisman to:
- relax and renew one's body (when hung in the bedroom)

Protects as an amulet against:
- possible harm to oneself and one's loved ones in one's home

GRIFFIN - *Vigilance and Resurrection*

The griffin consists of the body of a lion and the head of an eagle. Wings may also be attached to the lion's body as well as a tail, like the illustration. The griffin is a guard. It has been said that he is stronger than a hundred eagles and larger than eight lions. In Greece he was sacred to Apollo and Athena. His qualities are vigilance, power, and wisdom. In his most terrifying shape, he is a vengeful being. Medieval thinkers perceived in him a divine-human duality, like Christ's, assigning the eagle to the sky and the lion to the earth. Both the eagle and the lion are also associated with the sun and thus the griffin is a symbol for resurrection. The sun sets in the evenings to be reborn the next morning.

Helps as a talisman to:
- be confident and alert
- develop strength and be righteous

Protects as an amulet against:
- the darkness of the unconscious
- lack of vigilance

The Twelve Foundation Stones of Celestial Jerusalem

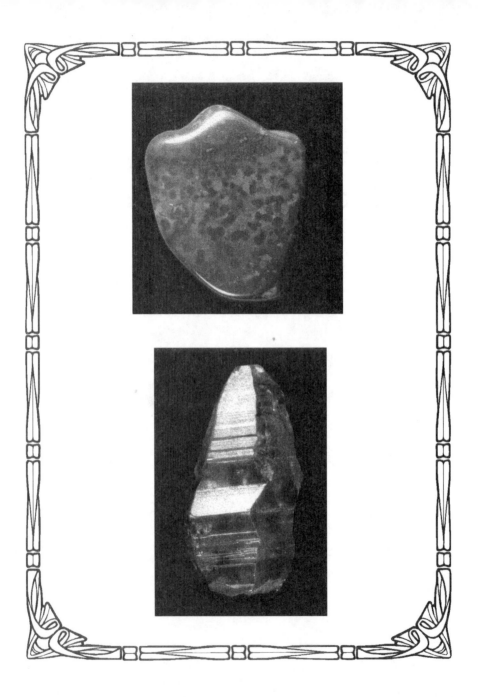

HELIOTROPE - *Blood Jasper* - *Vitality*

This is the first foundation stone from Celestial Jerusalem in the Book of Revelations. The heliotrope is a dark-green Chalcedon with red spots. In the Middle Ages, magical powers were attributed to this stone, because the red blotches represent the blood of Christ.

Helps as a talisman to:
- warm and rejuvenate the body
- lead a long life and look young
- concentrate spiritually and enhance wisdom

Protects as an amulet against:
- wounds, snake bites, scorpion stings
- enemies and illness
- nightmares and sleep disorders

Assignation: March / blister / hemorrhoids, wounds

SAPPHIRE - *Blue Corundum* - *Fidelity*

The second foundation stone from Celestial Jerusalem was known in the Middle Ages as lapis lazuli. The dark blue sapphire and the star sapphire are the characteristic stones. Blue is the color of fidelity; the star in the stone connects us with the universe. The sapphire strengthens faith and healing powers in man.

Helps as a talisman to:
- be steadfast in virtue
- remain faithful and true in marriage
- be healthy, intelligent, and rational

Protects as an amulet against:
- confusion and illusion
- strong outbreaks of rage or hysteria
- learning disabilities

Assignation: April / Sagittarius / Jupiter / hearts, lungs, kidneys / growths, gout, rashes, cold sweats, poison

CHALCEDON - *Contentment*

This is the third foundation stone from Celestial Jerusalem. The name Chalcedon goes back to an ancient city on the Bospherus. The stone is a milky blue and belongs to the quartzes. Its wave-like lines aid the flow of speech through the throat and vocal chords.

Helps as a talisman to:
- develop one's ability to speak publicly and eliminate speech defects
- maintain peace and calm
- attain inner contentment

Protects as an amulet against:
- weakness of spirit and depression
- the hypnotic powers of others
- nightmares and sleep disorders
- inhibitions and stage fright

Assignation: June / Sagittarius / gall

EMERALD - *Love*

The fourth foundation stone of Celestial Jerusalem, the emerald, is a light-green stone. Green Stone is the meaning of the Greek root of the word. It breaks out of stone with power and represents the force of growth. Its healing powers are best applied to the red illnesses such as inflammations, but it is also useful as an antidote to poison.

Helps as a talisman to:
- care for the eyes
- attain youthfulness and be happy
- make up and promote love and stability

Protects as an amulet against:
- the evil eye
- sin and temptation
- forgetfulness

Assignation: May / Cancer / the moon / eyes, heart / lack of appetite, epilepsy, fever, growths, hemorrhoids, headaches, insomnia, pregnancy, poison, worms

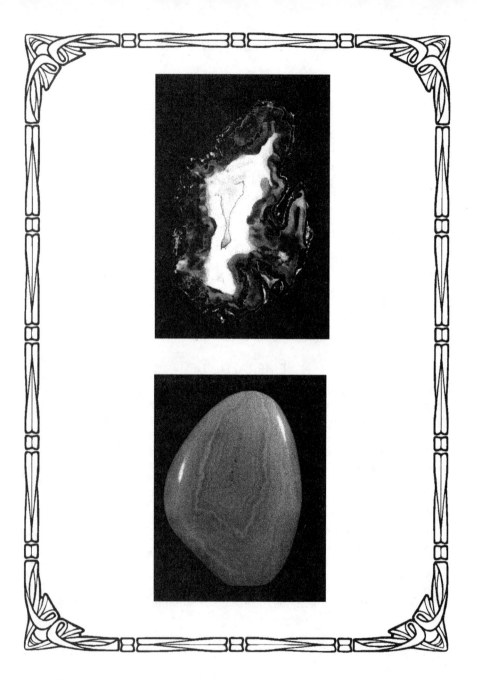

SARDONYX - *Friends*

The fifth stone of the Celestial Jerusalem, the Sardonyx, reveals the earth in its reddish-brown layers; it also contains the white Chalcedon stripes. It was once considered the gold of antiquity. It neutralizes poisonous bites and wounds, from both plant and insect, as well as poisonous stab wounds. Today, the Sardonyx is the stone for healing and protection.

Helps as a talisman to:
- increase one's self-confidence and self-control
- be happy in love and marriage
- bring to light the truth in legal matters

Protects as an amulet against:
- infections and relapses of illness
- false friends and the fear of the foreign
- all evil

Assignation: Capricorn / Saturn

SARDER - *Passion*

This is the sixth foundation stone of Celestial Jerusalem. The Sarder is a Chalcedon-like stone, whose reddish-brown color recalls fire. He is brought together with inspiration and passion.

Helps as a talisman to:
- maintain one's beauty
- cement friendships
- sharpen understanding

Protects as an amulet against:
- false love
- frigidity toward one's fellow man
- cowardice and morbidity

Assignation: Scorpion / Pluto / ears / high blood pressure, fever, headaches, pregnancy

CHRYSOLITH (PERIDOT) - *Balance*

The Chrysolith is the seventh stone of Celestial Jerusalem. It is a glass-green, transparent stone which reminds one of the lights that shines through the May foliage. It is often found in meteorites. Thus, many believe that it bears the quality of the sun in itself, having arisen from the sun's explosion. It has been used as a healing stone for centuries. Its name means "equal energy."

Helps as a talisman to:
- stabilize the immune system and the inner balance
- maintain the proper attitude toward life - open one's inner eye
- build better relations with one's fellow man - be successful at work

Protects as an amulet against:
- envy, egotism, and lack of emotion
- fury and jealousy
- sadness and feelings of being beaten

Assignation: August / Cancer / colon, stomach, kidneys / epilepsy, insomnia

BERYL - *Clairvoyance*

The eighth foundation stone in Celestial Jerusalem, beryl, is the source of the German "Braille" (eyeglasses). This refers to the colorless, transparent type of mineral. The magic stone affirms the faith in god. Through his lenses we can better see the spiritual world.

Helps as a talisman to:
- maintain love in marriage
- be charming and have sex appeal - stay young at heart
- increase erotic effects and find happiness

Protects as an amulet against:
- dangers on journeys
- homesickness and highway fever
- near-sightedness and myopia in life

Assignation: May / sun / glands / asthma, melancholy

PRECIOUS TOPAZ - *Purity*

Topaz, the ninth foundation stone of Celestial Jerusalem, is thought to protect the "city of gold" from demonic forces. Its white or light-blue transparency opens the senses to inspirations and connects the soul with the body. It heals poor eyesight.

Helps as a talisman to:
- strengthen true friendship and trust
- begin something new
- keep one's head screwed on and remain self-confident

Protects as an amulet against:
- sudden rage
- relapses to addictions
- risks upon which one might unexpectedly stumble
Assignation: November / Leo / Mercury / skin, heart / fever, hemorrhoids, vericose veins, thrombosis

CHYSOPRAS - *Fidelity*

The Greek name of the tenth foundation stone from Celestial Jerusalem, "gold leek," refers both to its glimmer and to its wonderful green color. Green connects use with the world of vegetation and its intrinsic elementary being. Its green is the symbol for the eternally young love. It has a calming effect on the circulation.

Helps as a talisman to:
- maintain love in marriage
- protect fidelity between lovers
- harbor hope for renewal
- demand the highest respect

Protects as an amulet against:
- black magic
- chaos and bad moods
- a lack of will power
Assignation: May / Cancer / heart, vessels / nausea, gout

HYACINTH - *Healing*

In antiquity, the eleventh foundation stone of Celestial Jerusalem, the hyacinth, was attributed the power to recognize the final truth. The yellowish-red to reddish-brown of the stone opens a perspective on the spiritual world beyond our own world. It is a very powerful healing stone.

Helps as a talisman to:
- undertake astral voyages
- gain human knowledge
- enter into a new partnership

Protects as an amulet against:
- being prejudicial
- feelings of inferiority
- static situations in life

Assignation: December / Venus / heart, lungs / metabolic disorders

AMETHYST - *Moderation*

The twelfth foundation stone from Celestial Jerusalem, the amethyst, is violet and effervescent. It joins us with the spiritual world. Violet is the last color in the spectrum and leads over into the invisible world of the infinite. Here, we are able to experience peace and harmony, devotion and the otherworldliness of our being.

Helps as a talisman to:
- enhance one's spirit of enterprise
- strengthen one's faith
- stimulate one's fantasy

Protects as an amulet against:
- learning disabilities and fear of tests
- alcoholism and its consequences
- false friends and homelessness

Assignation: February / Pisces / Jupiter / throat / venereal diseases, growths, hysteria, neuralgia, acne, insomnia, dropsy

The Western Zodiac

ARIES - *The Ram - Personality*

The forward-leaping ram breaks down every door and runs right at all opportunities. He has to test himself and stands for the new beginning and the nascent spring that follows the long winter.

Helps as a talisman to:
- develop one's personality and character
- be confident and ready to take risks
- feel excitement at the beginning of an event

Protects as an amulet against:
- becoming bogged down and mired in circumstances
- limitations
- anxieties

Assignation: red, reddish / fire / Mars / cornelian, red jasper, ruby / Native American medicine wheel of the bear tribe: red hawk (moon of the budding tree)

TAURUS - *The Bull - Possession*

The bull is bound to the earth and sedentary. He wants to possess the earth, which he works and transforms into fertile fields. He is thorough in his work and acts according to tradition. Hence, he is afraid of the new and tries to protect himself by keeping a stiff neck.

Helps as a talisman to:
- strengthen fertility
- develop sensuality
- not overvalue reality

Protects as an amulet against:
- existential angst
- moodiness, depression
- violence

Assignation: pink, bright red, orange / earth / Venus / Achat, cornelian, rose quartz, rhodonie, rhodochrosite / Native American medicine wheel of the bear tribe: beaver (moon of the returning frogs)

GEMINI - *The Twins - Reason*

Twins need the other to recognize themselves. They inquire into their surroundings. The knowledge gained is processed by their reason and passed on again to their surroundings. At least two are always required for an exchange.

Helps as a talisman to:
- overcome communication difficulties
- prove one's objectivity
- change opinions and stand behind them

Protects as an amulet against:
- exaggerations
- slips of the tongue
- difficulty in making contacts

Assignation: yellow, orange / air / Mercury / amber, citrine, gold topaz / Native American medicine wheel of the bear tribe: deer (moon of the seed sown in May)

CANCER - *The Crab - Feelings*

This illustration shows the crab's affectionate nature. He has no elbows. His ability to get his way lies in the gentle motto: the steady drip wears away the stone. He wants to feel at one with his home and workplace. If attacked, he steps aside.

Helps as a talisman to:
- have and project a sense of security
- give oneself over to daydreams and find spiritual power in meditation
- let one's emotions have free rein

Protects as an amulet against:
- hypersensitivity
- mood swings
- spiritual injuries

Assignation: green / water / the Moon / aventurine, crystal, chrysopras, Peridot, emerald / Native American medicine wheel of the bear tribe: sparrow (moon of the burning sun)

LEO - *The Lion - Love*

Powerful and with a feeling of sheer force, the lion strides through the heat of summer. He affirms life and does it with a loud roar and a flick of his tail. He draws attention to himself and is convinced of his uniqueness.

Helps as a talisman to:
- gain luxury goods and to distribute them generously
- radiate a warmth of heart and improve one's love life
- develop power and courage

Protects as an amulet against:
- exaggerated pride
- poverty and hunger
- being a wallflower

Assignation: white, gold / fire / the Sun / rock crystal, diamond, precious topaz / Native American medicine wheel of the bear tribe: sturgeon (moon of ripe berries)

VIRGO - *The Virgin - Health*

The main characteristic of this sign is caution. The Virgo proceeds methodically, at an even pace. Sometimes, they even take a step back after a risky move. This results in the indecisiveness of the sign. Should I or shouldn't I? The Virgo analyzes everything and is happiest when saying: I knew that.

Helps as a talisman to:
- be conscientious and careful in evaluations
- maintain one's health and ability to work
- be protected in all of life's many circumstances

Protects as an amulet against:
- chaos and zealotry
- lack of care
- illness and allergies

Assignation: yellow, yellow-gold, orange / earth / Mercury / citrine, gold topaz, tiger's eye / Native American medicine wheel of the bear tribe: brown bear

LIBRA - *The Scales - Partnership*

The symbol for Libra is a scale balanced. The Libra tries to always be the straight arrow and well balanced. This makes him constantly weigh matters and plan things. He cannot bear too little or too much; justice is his first commandment. Libra looks at both sides and attempts to be fair to all. When decisions need to be made, Libra is therefore often poor at making them.

Helps as a talisman to:
- lead to reconciliation
- act justly
- create a true partnership of equals

Protects as an amulet against:
- indecision
- glorifying over-ambition
- confused thoughts

Assignation: blue, greenish, brown, white / air / Venus / green tourmaline, jade, obsidian, smoky quartz / Native American medicine wheel of the bear tribe: raven (moon of migrating geese)

SCORPIO - *The Scorpion - Sexuality*

At first Scorpio is methodical, like Virgo; then with a huge leap, Scorpio transcends all norms and taboos. This leap can take the form of passion but can also be a form of self-immolation for the good of community. This self image, however, is often just an ideal, a figment present only in his imagination. Scorpio seeks out the spiritual order in all creation and expunges the old with his stinger.

Helps as a talisman to:
- establish principles and pursue ideals
- develop a sense of sacrifice
- overcome oneself and to exhibit endurance

Protects as an amulet against:
- fanaticism and blind faith
- a lack of emotion
- the fear of death

Assignation: red, reddish, blackish-red / water / Pluto / hematite, cornelian, red tourmaline / Native American medicine wheel of the bear tribe: snake

SAGITTARIUS- *The Archer - Education*

The archer aims for the sky. He is one with the bow and target. He wants to fly, like his arrow, far away, learning about everything and pursuing new goals. His dynamism is as well known is his thirst for knowledge.

Helps as a talisman to:
- satisfy one's desire for knowledge
- develop one's understanding and powers of persuasion
- travel to distant countries and to understand foreign races

Protects as an amulet against:
- boredom
- spiritual bankruptcy
- the perils of travel

Assignation: blue / fire / Jupiter / Chalcedon, lapis lazuli, sodalith, sapphire/ Native American medicine wheel of the bear tribe: Wapiti (moon of the long snow)

CAPRICORN - *The Goat - Prestige*

The goat leaps over the most treacherous cliffs and walks confidently on the flat ground. Thoroughness is his highest commandment. He is obdurate and lives according to his own laws, which he is pleased to foist upon others. Like the symbol, his thoughts are directed toward the past and to the study of tradition in archaeology and history. He buries himself with some bitterness in his duties, often forgetting the joy of life.

Helps as a talisman to:
- develop endurance and be thorough
- exhibit humor at work
- pursue one's calling

Protects as an amulet against:
- danger while mountain climbing
- false career aims
- the errors of youth

Assignation: green, black / earth / Saturn / malachite, moss agate, onyx, Sardonyx, black tourmaline / Native American medicine wheel of the bear tribe: snow goose (moon of the earth's rejuvenation)

AQUARIUS - *The Water Bearer - Freedom*

This may be the ancient Egyptian symbol for water, but Aquarius is an air sign, comparable to the breeze that ruffles the surface of the ocean. He can, however, also be like a hurricane that drives the ocean's waves ever higher. Aquarius is spontaneous and free-spirited. Like the wind, he refuses to be fit into a mold; he prefers to float above things.

Helps as a talisman to:
- live free and easy
- live in harmony with all things
- demand one's freedom

Protects as an amulet against:
- egotism
- lack of imagination
- being caught up in the past

Assignation: blue, turquoise, green / air / Uranus / ammonite, aquamarine, turquoise / Native American medicine wheel of the bear tribe: otter (moon of respite and cleansing)

PISCES - *The Fish - Secret*

Two fish are swimming in the water. They look at one another and pass each other by. They are agile in their liquid element, but their sphere of life also traps them. Since fish do not need a ground upon which to travel or to propel them, real life is a burden to them. They dream while swimming and feel the pull of the unconscious. Pisces does not look to defend itself but flees instead into this unworldly state.

Helps as a talisman to:
- meditate and dream
- develop empathy and selflessness
- uncover secrets

Protects as an amulet against:
- large, dangerous animals
- noise and unrest
- being discovered

Assignation: violet, blue / water / Neptune / amethyst, fluorite, opal, moonstone, sugilith / Native American medicine wheel of the bear tribe: puma

Maya

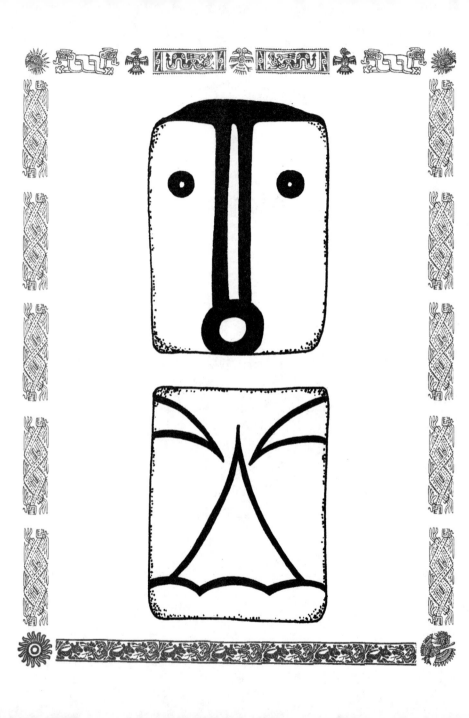

AHAU - *Love - Union*

The union is depicted through identical parts that together form a whole. The round symbol below represents the cosmic harmony that arises when two parts come together as a whole. Through true union we attain solar mastery, no longer losing ourselves in idle egotism but giving ourselves over to ecstasy.

Helps as a talisman to:
- embody love
- learn the art of acceptance and toleration
- feel the sacred within oneself

Protects as an amulet against:
- expectations in love
- value judgments
- conditional love

Assignation: gold / passion flower, sunflower / amber / gold topaz, yellow sapphire / fire / south

AKBAL - *Dream - Dream Time*

This symbol sends us into a sacred sleep, in which things from the hidden world can arise. We turn our gaze within and begin a voyage into ourselves. This brings us into connection with holiness and the mysteries. The end result is uplifted spirits because we come to know even our shadow. We can inquire into our dreams with this symbol and come into connection with our ancestors and previous lives, in order to gain knowledge and capacities for the present.

Helps as a talisman to:
- know oneself and become conscious
- count one's own mistakes as important learning steps
- recognize inner qualities and to bring them out

Protects as an amulet against:
- one-dimensionality
- depression and self-criticism
- fear of change

Assignation: black / wormwood, poppy, black orchid / auroma resin / obsidian, smoky quartz, onyx, hematite / water / west

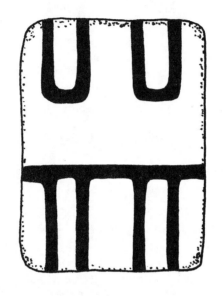

BEN - *Courage - Angel Messenger*

This symbol stands for perseverance in spite of danger, which is symbolized by the upper teeth. Below, one finds the straight path on earth. The border points to the unknown. We are the time-space travelers who move on a secret journey through the worlds and eras. When we come up against the unknown, we have also overcome the danger; we find ourselves in a heavenly place from which our sympathy, born of courage, can flow.

Helps as a talisman to:
- radiate courage and sympathy
- think of life as a sacred voyage
- strike out in new directions

Protects as an amulet against:
- the fear of the unknown
- exaggerated shyness
- the strong desire for solitude

Assignation: red of dusk / almond, clove, pink rose / rose scent / rose quartz / Rosa sapphire / earth / east

CABAN - *Orientation - Shield*

This symbol suggests that one can find one's center either through a twisting path or a straight path. Both figures, the serpentine spiral and the dotted line, stand for the same event and attitude. They express the earth's power and the search for traces. These are the earth's protectors and they govern the healing power of crystals.

Helps as a talisman to:
- live in the present
- observe without drawing conclusions
- remember that we live on earth to take part in an extraordinary process of development

Protects as an amulet against:
- living in the past or future and losing oneself in signs, symbols, dreams, or visions
- drawing too hasty conclusions
- not feeling at home in one's earthly body

Assignation: purple-red / fuchsia, ginger, Easter pink / Nag Champa / dark pink tourmaline, morganite (pink beryl) / earth / east

CAUAC - *Purification - Union*

The illustration shows the breakdown of borders and the reunion of two separated bodies that belong together. Recognition that they belong together leads to a transformation and ultimately to the ecstasy of freedom.

Helps as a talisman to:
- connect with the inner self
- connect two separated people
- overcome growth pains

Protects as an amulet against:
- profound despair and addictive behavior
- physical calcification and repression
- the fear of the unknown
Assignation: royal purple / garlic, vervain / incense, myrrh / sugilith, violet fluorite / water / west

CHICCHAN - *Enthusiasm - Passion*

An open eye and a smile helps one to deal with things. The lips project sensuality and vitality. The head is covered with a cap, demonstrating the predominance of instincts and feelings. This attitude creates worlds.

Helps as a talisman to:
- experience a higher consciousness through passion and physicality
- be in harmony with one's higher consciousness
- make decisions instinctively

Protects as an amulet against:
- decisions based on convention
- pure physicality and the desires of the senses
- the failure to recognize instinctive truth
Assignation: orange red / cardamom, cayenne, poppy, gladioli / musk / cornelian, fire agate, red coral / earth / east

CHUEN - *Innocence - Humor*

The physical eyes are closed, but the third eye is wide open. Like a flower, the mouth is agape, holding a pearl between the lips. Silently, this pure face floats on the surface of the original sea of creation, like a child, who suddenly raises his voice and speaks the truth in all innocence.

Helps as a talisman to:
- speak openly and in truth
- develop refined emotions
- meet life and its demands with humor

Protects as an amulet against:
- being too serious
- those who would damage joy - mockery of others
- lack of refinement in feeling and the bite of scorn
Assignation: aquamarine blue / blueberry, mint, daisy / cinnamon / aquamarine, turquoise / water / west

CIB - *The Inner Voice - Understanding*

The inner voice glides upward and almost fills the entire room. By listening to this voice and its message, we are able to climb the heavenly ladder and receive the mystical word of God. The ears are on either side. The third eye is open toward the sky. The beam of understanding glides back and forth providing thus for the exchange.

Helps as a talisman to:
- establish the link to the divine and create the inner voice
- develop faith in one's own mystical intelligence
- understand one's world

Protects as an amulet against:
- insensitivity
- ignoring one's inner voice
- failing to acknowledge a spiritual destiny
Assignation: indigo blue, gold / clover / honeysuckle / double-ended quartz / fire / south

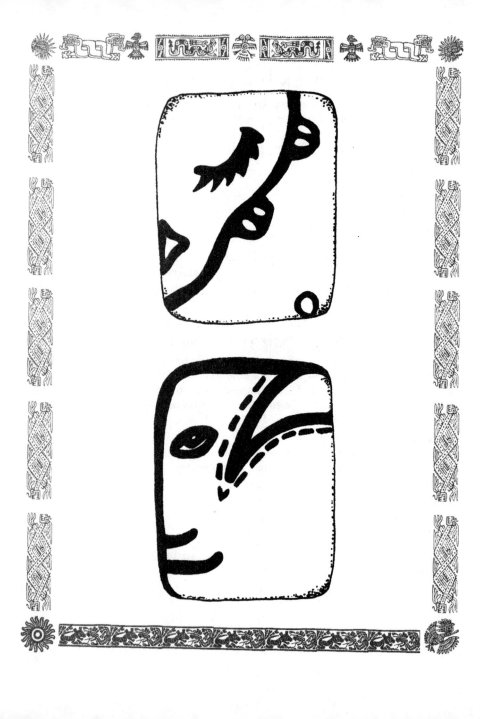

CIMI - *Death - Liberation*

The picture shows a peaceful, sleeping face, where one can see the sweetness of its experience. It appears to have thrown off all earthly cares and limitations. A withdrawal from earthly customs and the gift of the body to the eternally same can be recognized in the calm composure of the expression.

Helps as a talisman to:
- become humble and serene
- forgive
- renounce control of one's spiritual development

Protects as an amulet against:
- the fear of death
- being alone in difficult times
- struggle and resistance
Assignation: forest green / catnip, heather / gardenia / malachite, jade, emerald, moss agate / air / north

EB - *Grass - Excess*

The illustration shows a face, that has one eye is open and looking upward. Inspiration is poured in different steps into the mind, which is open like a goblet. This enlivens the face. It is the spirit of live in all plants and organic life; it is the excess from the universe, which fills the vessel here.

Helps as a talisman to:
- do good for oneself
- empty the mind in order to become a channel for cosmic consciousness
- acknowledge one's body as a means of transformation

Protects as an amulet against:
- inadequacy
- acting purely based on reason
- underestimation of the mind
Assignation: light bronze / ginger, brunelle / apple blossom scent / topaz, ritual quartz / fire / south

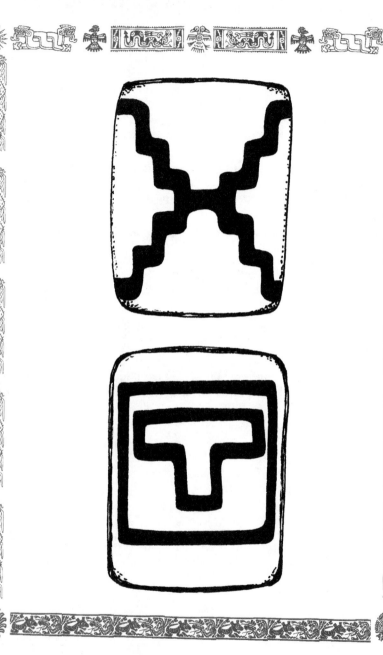

ETZNAB - *Flint - Discernment*

The two sides reflect each other but so do top and bottom. One cannot tell which is the original image; all four determine each other. By penetrating all the reflections, one comes to truth: it can only be attained in a complete void. In the absence of time one experiences lucidity and becomes a spiritual warrior, who bears the sword of truth before him and sees his shadow in his eye.

Helps as a talisman to:
- recognize deceptions in life
- accept truths even when they are difficult
- see the other reality

Protects as an amulet against:
- illusions
- feelings separated from others
- judging and being judged; value judgments
Assignation: silver / sage, pomegranate, orchid / lemon, green mint / diamond, silver-colored pyrite / air / north

IK - *The Wind - Inspiration*

The vital spirit moves in a simple form, a simple body. Its bright light pours into man and enlivens him as an invisible power. The three lines indicate the three-dimensionality of earthly life: height, breadth, and depth. Suddenly, at the same time, the spirit breathes in all three dimensions. Thus this symbol stands for both the present and simplicity.

Helps as a talisman to:
- know the source of inspiration
- act according to inspiration
- view oneself as a living, whole creation

Protects as an amulet against:
- feeling separate from creation
- the need to criticize
- feeling alone
Assignation: transparency, white light / eucalyptus, herbs, lily / copal resin / diamond, quartz / air / north

IMIX - *Aboriginal Water - Receptivity*

The wise dragon arises out of the aboriginal water, where the whirlpool draws its eternal spirals. Its four feelers stand for the original trust and stability found in the water, which provides him with a constant source of nourishment. Above him, the sun shines, giving rise to life in the aboriginal waters.

Helps as a talisman to:
- have faith in the divine source
- achieve what one wants
- communicate to others one's feelings, dreams, and desires

Protects as an amulet against:
- giving with the expectation of receiving something in return
- the desire for guarantees and insurance
- the need for confirmation and recognition
Assignation: burgundy / nettle, dark brown carnation, and rose / cedar, sage / garnet, hematite, ruby / earth / east

IX - *Jaguar - Shaman*

On the glimmering underground, all seeing eyes swim. Their paths lead constantly upwards to divine knowledge and the connection with god's will, until the latter becomes one with the individual's will. Transparency makes us the recipients of pure magic, which can flow through us and illuminate us. A natural equilibrium arises in us and makes us the mediator between worlds.

Helps as a talisman to:
- open oneself to magic and the joy of life
- be initiated into endless secrets
- enhance and practice shaman abilities

Protects as an amulet against:
- competitive thinking and the will to control
- the need for acknowledgment
- human frailty
Assignation: mother of pearl / basil, lily / patchouli / opal, crystal ball, green tourmaline / air / north

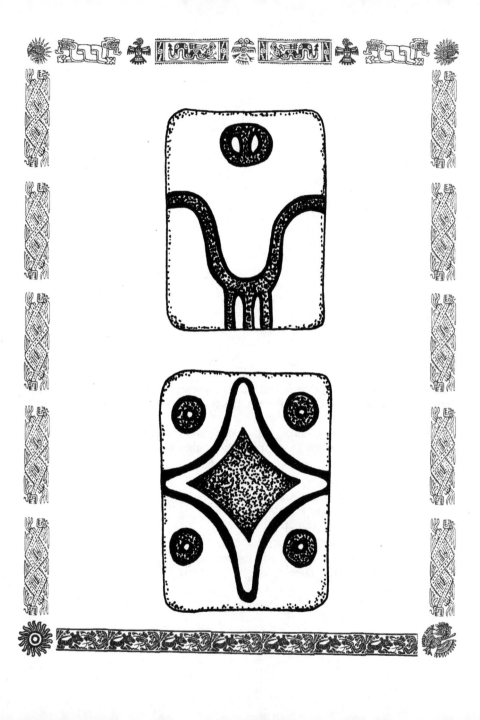

KAN - *Mais* - *Creation*

From the fertile earth, the seedling sprouts upward to meet its destiny. Three forces keep it bound to the earth, but it is open to the spiritual. New possibilities arise that must be filled with life so that they can blossom.

Helps as a talisman to:
- realize that one is able to create everything from itself
- free oneself from binding certainties
- turn dreams and desires into wishes

Protects as an amulet against:
- the fear of risk
- rigid thought patterns
- not trusting oneself

Assignation: saffron yellow / sunflower, dandelion, calendula / sapphron / citrine, golden tiger's eye / fire / south

LAMAT - *All-Encompassing Love* - *Harmony*

The large star stands in the middle of planets and points to many other stars in the infinity of space. Its form is that of complete harmony. In spite of varying energies everything in space moves in harmony. The star, in harmony with the planets, is a guiding light; it is the star of the south.

Helps as a talisman to:
- give love and remove all eliminate all incongruities from one's life
- live in the present
- find the right path to oneself and to others

Protects as an amulet against:
- self-doubt
- inhibitions against oneself
- unrealistic ideas

Assignation: blue of the evening sky and gold / Leg wave, sword lily, leek / jasmine scent / lapis lazuli, star sapphire / fire / south

MANIK - *Portal - Beauty*

The thumb and the four fingers of the hand create an opening through which we can see the clear, bright heavens above. A star glitters between the grasping fingers. In order to comprehend something, we must first be able to grasp it and see it in full light. Spiritual tools can, likewise, entrap the spirit of truth and beauty and thus serve as a portal to fulfillment.

Helps as a talisman to:
- finish things one has begun
- recognize resistance and distractions as such and eliminate them
- reach clear decisions

Protects as an amulet against:
- high pressure and being overburdened
- the fear of working with tools of whatever type
- the malice of the object

Assignation: gray-blue / blue aster, blue chrysanthemum, cornflower / tobacco / blue sapphire, blue quartz, moonstone / water / west

MEN - *Eagle - Hope*

The upturned face with feathers on the head looks upon divinity with open eyes. Like an eagle it rises up to receive the pure power of the divine and to shake off the limitations of daily life. Its thought is not centered on the "I" but is directed toward the all-encompassing.

Helps as a talisman to:
- gather one's powers
- increase one's faith in oneself
- know one's self-imposed duties

Protects as an amulet against:
- the feeling of always having to help
- not being able to say no
- the sense of lost love

Assignation: lavender / nutmeg, heather, elder / lavender scent / amethyst / water / west

MULUC - *Raindrops - Divine Intervention*

Water pours down from the sky either as a thick stream or as a light rain. It makes us aware of god's hand at work, giving meaning to life on earth. One's understanding of the power of life grows as one recalls who one is. In this way, the single raindrop becomes a third eye and the way between the streams of water a ladder to divine knowledge.

Helps as a talisman to:
- receive divine intervention
- reach cosmic understanding
- show one's light and to find support from others

Protects as an amulet against:
- self-denigrating talk
- nonsense
- resistance to a higher fate

Assignation: cherry red / estrogen, yellow root, amaryllis / lotus scent / quartz obelisk, cherry-colored agate / earth / east

OC - *Dog - New Beginning*

A laughing face looks out upon the world. It licks its upper lip with its tongue, like a dog that has eaten well. The three stripes represent the connection between man and his totem animals. It is closely linked to the animals; they lie against his body as one can see from the naked bosom in the upper right-hand corner.

Helps as a talisman to:
- make a connection with one's totems and familiars
- build and deepen relations to other humans
- find the dual soul of one's soul mate

Protects as an amulet against:
- jealousy and possessiveness
- a one-sided perspective
- loneliness

Assignation: peacock blue / magic nut, raspberry, narcissus, blue pine / rosemary oil / crystal, azurite, blue tourmaline / air / north

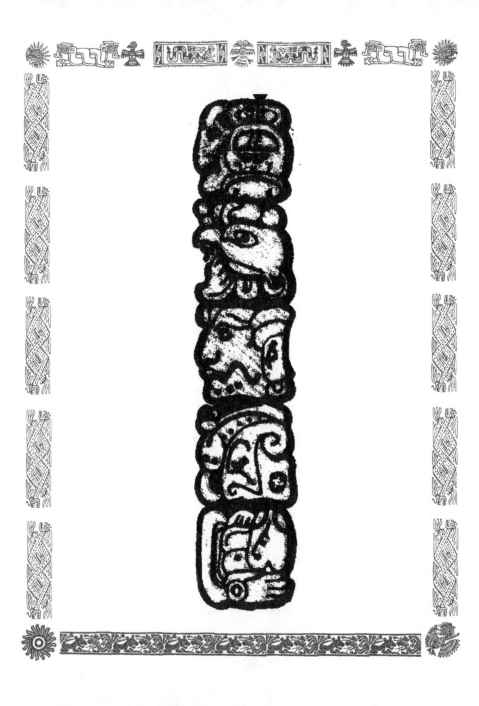

MAYA GLYPHS - *The Holy Scripture*

The ancient Mayans wrote using hieroglyphs. Like the Egyptians, the Maya decorated their temples with the history of their people. The hieroglyph had spiritual as well as aesthetic significance. The adjoining amulet is based on an inscription found on the great steps of the Quiche Maya in the western highlands of Guatemala. The Quiche were historically inclined and chiseled their past in stone; they are the source of the holy book, the Popul Vuh, in which their history and culture are documented.

Helps as a talisman to:
- understand the messages behind all forms of culture and their arts
Protects as an amulet against:
- darkness and delusion
- forgetfulness

Fetish Animals

of the North American Southwest

Fetish animals can protect us and help us with certain tasks. Find an animal whose characteristics suit those of your goal, and call upon it to help you. Through your request, you lend him the power to effectively support you.

BEAR - *Shash (n)* * - *Insight and Hindsight*

The bear is a very human and very powerful being. Its grace and prowess are praised in many legends. The bear is considered the father of the human race; it is the intermediary between heaven and earth because it sleeps deep in its cave, gathering insight and understanding. Because of this sleep, it is also associated with the moon: the bear "comes and goes." The backward-glancing bear reminds us of the old truths that we can still hear if we listen with our heart. This gaze into the past reminds us of where we come from and of our ancestors and our children who accompany us on the path of life. The bear wants to remind us of this. The Lakota Native Americans have a saying, "Mitakuye owasin," which means, "We are all related to each other."

Helps as a talisman to:
- find our way into the past and future
- know our destiny
- achieve the power and health of a bear

Protects as an amulet against:
- anorexia and fainting
- rootlessness

BUFFALO - *Ayání* * *Tatanka* ** - *Plentitude*

The massive buffalo stands for respect and material well-being. He was the main form of sustenance for many Native American tribes. The list of all his many useable parts would easily take up three pages of this book. The extermination of the buffalo was the end of the culture for those Native Americans who resided in the Great Plains. The buffalo is, however, still today the symbol of power, endurance, and plenitude. He fulfills all our needs. A life of plenty is at hand when the buffalo appears. We accept his gifts with gratitude.

Helps as a talisman to:
- bring plentitude into our lives, physically and spiritually
- develop more endurance and power
- keep grounded and to value the small things in life

Protects as an amulet against:
- hunger, poverty, and cold
- an unwillingness to work

*n = Navajo
**l = Lakota (Sioux language)

HORSE - *lii (n); Sunka tanka (l) - Freedom*

The horse was the most important animal for almost all Native American tribes. When the horse arrived in America with the Spanish, a prosperous time followed for the Native Americans. The horse made life in general easier, and, in particular, hunting buffalo easier. For the nomadic tribes of the Southwest, like the Apaches and the Navajo, stealing horses from neighboring tribes became a sport. The horse is a brave, fast animal and the symbol of freedom. The Lakota called it "the secret one" (wakan). It is linked to the soul and the Great Spirit.

Helps as a talisman to:
- develop courage and speed
- achieve freedom
- delve into one's unconscious and emotions

Protects as an amulet against:
- inhibition and limitation
- feeling downtrodden and against pessimism
- spiritual blocks

FISH - *Lóó (n) - Dreams and Visions*

In arid desert regions, the fish is the symbol for life-giving water. It illustrates how one can swim with the current, avoiding hindrances. The fish takes the opportunities he is given. It is good at perceiving and evaluating situations. The fish brings good luck and a long life. We should learn from it to consider our journey through life as an adventure. The fish will carry us into the realm of dreams and visions.

Helps as a talisman to:
- recall one's dreams and thereby to gain contact to one's soul
- acknowledge visions as actual events and to pursue them
- respond to opportunity when it calls
- value water as the origin of life

Protects as an amulet against:
- trying to break down the wall with one's head
- contempt for everything metaphysical

EAGLE - *Atsá (n); Wambli (l) - Divine Messenger*

In the Southwest, the eagle is the symbol of the messenger sent by god. The Hopi take a few young eagles from their nests in February and bring them to their villages They are pampered until July. They are given morsels of meat and colorful toys while they live on the roofs of the pueblo-like houses. In the summer, the eagles are sacrificed in a ceremony using Kachina shrines to carry them to their graves. They should tell the gods about man and intervene for him.

Helps as a talisman to:
- call upon higher beings for assistance
- commit one's worries to divine powers and to find solutions

Protects as an amulet against:
- crises of faith
- damage by lightning

OWL - *Warning*

In the Southwest, the owl is the bird of warning. If a village were befallen by contamination, Apache and Navajo tribes would place clay owls in the outlying trees as a form of warning to returning hunters or warriors. When an owl crosses our path at night, it is trying to warn us of threatening dangers.

Helps as a talisman to:
- recognize dangers early on and to take the necessary preventative measures
- decipher inexplicable premonitions
- find our way at night or in unclear circumstances

Protects as an amulet against:
- night blindness

SNAKE - *The Little Brother - Rebirth*

The snake molts and casts off its skin once it has fulfilled its duties. It is constantly changing, and passionate until death. Depending on the circumstance, the snake is quiet and hypnotizes its enemy, or it strikes like lightning and bites with its poisonous fangs. The snake's passion is closely linked to its blood lust. This is why the climax in lovemaking is known as the "little death." Here, we are closest to the Great Spirit. In the pueblos, the snake summons thunder and lightning, which bring rain and nourish the earth, ensuring a good harvest. The snake in this case is a symbol for the flash, which is a product of its slithering form.

Helps as a talisman to:
- transform oneself and to go a step further
- not allow any compromises in love
- recognize and take advantage of the right moment

Protects as an amulet against:
- snake bites
- lightning strikes

LIZARD – DREAM TIME

The lizard seeks out the sun and warmth, just as the soul of man seeks consciousness. The lizard dreams, and in this state, he becomes one with the dreamtime and its many possibilities. It represents the infinite cosmos and the art of living out one's dreams, that is, the art of creating one's own world.

Helps as a talisman to:
- make dreams come true
- enhance one's fantasy and to be artistic
- enjoy the day, the sun, and the warmth; to create a free space in which one can live out one's dreams

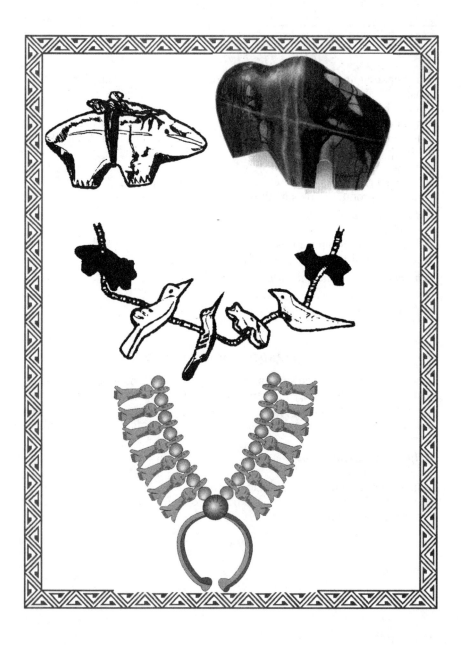

FETISH ANIMALS AND FETISH NECKLACES

Stone animals are associated with certain powers belonging to the real animal. As a fetish animal, it provides the bearer with the corresponding qualities or protects him or her from attacks by man, animal, or evil spirits. The animals are still carved from soapstone, semi-precious stones, or other stones. They are bound to the power of the stones. On the far left, one sees a bear; on the right, a buffalo made of onyx. Below, there is an illustration of a fetish necklace with birds, bears, and coyotes.

Helps as a talisman to:
- commune with animals and to request their aid
- experience the powers of these animals and to protect oneself from attacks

Protects as an amulet against:
- hunger (buffalo), frailty (bear), sadness (bird), betrayal (coyote)

PUMPKIN BLOSSOM NECKLACE WITH NAJA

This type of chain was much loved by the ancient Romans. Women wore it to come into contact with the feminine powers of the moon, which could enhance beauty, feminine wisdom, and feelings. Later, the moon-shaped pendant in the middle bore a cross at its center, representing the earth. For Christians, this necklace symbolized the church. The Romans, on the other hand, hung this moon around the necks of their horses to ensure a safe journey, and the Spaniards brought it to the "New World." The Navajo and the Apache liked this necklace so much that they integrated it into their own ceremonial jewelry. They decorated the pearl chain with silvery pumpkin blossoms, symbolizing fertility. The half moons are known as Naja or Najahe. They stand for the love and beauty that are the basic desire of all Navajo.

Totem Spirits

of the American Northwest and
the sub-arctic regions

The word "totem" comes from the Algonquin Native Americans and means relation or protective spirit. In the mystical imagination, totem spirits represent the common destiny of man and animal. The totem animal counts as a forbear and animal double enjoys taboo, which means, it cannot be hunted or eaten. Totem spirits protect the person who honors them as one would the members of one's family.

TOTEM POLE - *Holy Protection*

The totem pole is a symbol of protection for many tribes of the Northwest, who live along the Pacific coast. Images of animals, whose special powers set them apart, are carved into the massive tree trunks along with the faces of ancestors. The ancestors serve as a link between the tribe or clan and its past. The totem pole was erected to protect the land and its legacy. The upper-most animal is often an eagle (vision and protection) or a raven (power of transformation). The souls of the birds were thought to be at home both in the sky and on the earth; they could exert their powers in either world. Sacrifices were laid before the totem pole to honor the dead and to unite the clan.

Helps as a talisman to:
- join with animal and ancestors, receiving their power

Protects as an amulet against:
- inner and outer dangers

SOUL CATCHER

This so-called "soul catcher" belonged to a shaman of one of the Tsimshian Native American tribes. It is made of bone, oyster shell, and leather. It was used by the shaman on his spiritual trips. When the spirit of the dying had already left the body and was on its way to the realm of the dead, the shaman sought, with the help of this amulet, to catch the soul and bring it back. The amulet can be used not only to catch souls but it also protects the soul and brings it back safely.

THE SUN - *Light*

The sun's warmth and light makes fruit grow and gives us life. The sun lives in the house of the Great Spirit and distributes his gifts. In the north, the sun's time in the sky is precious. Darkness reins almost half a year in the north. The people wait for the sun and its blessings.

Helps as a talisman to:
- bring light into the darkness
- gather new powers of life
- greet each new day with joy and to carry out even the smallest labor with joy

Protects as an amulet against:
- depression, lack of joy, and fear of the next day

THE SPINNING WHEEL - *Eternally Same Motion*

The little man is the earth spirit. As the guardian of the heavens, he bears the totem pole in his mouth. Around it, the world turns. He watches over the eternally same motion, and eternal change in the higher worlds and on earth. He shows us that even as little people we can keep the whole world in motion once we have discovered our equilibrium.

Helps as a talisman to:
- find one's equilibrium
- have all situations under control
- not underestimate oneself

Protects as an amulet against:
- the changing conditions of life and against being swept up by them
- uncertainty
- a one-dimensional point of view

THE WARRIOR - *Deliberate Action*

Because they were the defenders of the tribe or clan, the warriors were highly esteemed. A warrior's whole body was trained to react immediately to danger, and his spirit was in harmony with his body. He made decisions and led the clan on its wanderings. When uncertain, he turned to the wisdom of the eagle, the vision of the falcon, and the leadership of the wolf, in order to find the right path again. His life was absolute consciousness.

Helps as a talisman to:
- develop spiritual leadership and self-accountability
- achieve a steadfastness of body and peace of mind
- act in cold-blood in dangerous situations

Protects as an amulet against:
- attacks
- uncertainties
- indecision

THE GREETING - *Openness*

The raised hand facing outward is a gesture of peace, friendship, and congeniality known around the world. By showing both hands openly, we demonstrate that we bear no weapons or ill will. Our hearts are as open as our hands.

Helps as a talisman to:
- cement friendships
- be open to all people in this world
- set aside disputes

Protects as an amulet against:
- enemies
- stinginess and cold-heartedness
- xenophobia

THE EAGLE - *Lucidity*

Like the tribes of the southwest, the Native Americans of the northwest, such as Tlingit, Kwakiutl, and Tsimshian, valued the eagle. The eagle stands in direct connection to the Great Spirit. When a warrior donned eagle feathers, it was a sign that he had grasped the essentials of life and identified himself with the strength of the eagle god. A whole headband was the symbol of the thunderbird and thus of the universal spirit, each feather representing a ray of sunlight.

Helps as a talisman to:
- attain a higher level of understanding
- consider things from a higher perspective and be thus above them
- know one's own strengths and to feel at one with the Great Spirit

THE RAVEN - *Magic*

The raven has many qualities in common with the Great Spirit. It has magical powers and can transform itself. The aboriginal peoples tell of its ability to cast spells. He teaches us to live deliberately, with humility and in moderation. Some Native American tribes thought the raven created the world. He carried pebbles in his beak, let them fall over the sea, and made the first islands.

Helps as a talisman to:
- foresee future events
- recognize dangers and to avoid them through change
- be more modest in one's lifestyle

Protects as an amulet against:
- spells and black magic

THE OWL - *Astral Journeys*

The owl created the night and is thus a symbol for wisdom, lucidity, and astral projection. Its magic accompanies its moonless flight and silent hunt. Its sharp vision shows it the way to higher knowledge. For many Native Americans, the owl was an uncanny creature. Because it hunts at night, it is, therefore, in possession of qualities not belonging to mankind.

Helps as a talisman to:
- be clear-sighted and to send one's astral body on journeys
- see in the dark; to develop a sixth sense
- become wise through visions

Protects as an amulet against:
- blindness
- too strong a connection to the body
- the fear of darkness

THE WHALE - *Origin*

The whale is the familiar spirit that knows the story of the ancient motherland that sank into the sea. The whale sings its songs in ever-changing patterns. In this way, the ancient stories are passed on to us and kept real.

Helps as a talisman to:
- learn from old tales and to profit therefrom
- expose repressed matter in the deepest layer of the unconscious
- acknowledge the beauty of our soul

THE WHALE SPIRIT - *Beneficence*

The whale was to the Native Americans of the Northwest what the buffalo was to the Plains Native Americans. Its body provided sustenance, clothing, cooking oil, and bones for implements. The goddess of the sea, Sedna, is the whale's protector.

The whale is a powerful totem animal. Ritual and shaman artifacts are often decorated with whales. The whale hunt was a holy rite, in which the kill was reserved for only a few hunters. The aboriginal tribes often carved talismans out of respect and gratitude. These objects helped them to feel at ease in a strange environment and endowed them with the assurance that life's essentials such as food, clothing, and warmth were on hand. With the whale's help we can receive endless gifts while, at the same time, being generous to others.

ORCA - *Emotions*

This, too, is an animal of the whale's protector Sedna, the mother of the deep. The Orca is proud and faithful, the keeper of secrets. When we call upon him, we can take part in the wisdom of the water.

Helps as a talisman to:
- stand behind our feelings and be proud of the wealth of our emotions
- maintain fidelity
- develop a sense of public spirit

THE FROG - *Purification*

The frog is a rain singer for the Northwest Native Americans. The rain cleanses the rivers and lakes, the houses and man. It renews the environment. The frog is the sacred spirit of renewal. Soft tears wash over the emotions. All holy waters belong to the frog. The body and the soul become clear and purified.

Helps as a talisman to:
- explain feelings and to free oneself of old spiritual impurities
- renew oneself in water

Protects as an amulet against:
- impurities of the body, thoughts, or feelings and the soul

THE SEAL - *Fortuitous Travel*

Each year the seal and its companions cross thousands of miles of ocean. Only the large numbers guarantee safety. When we travel, we should surround ourselves with like-minded people, who want to reach the same goal. This applies to trips undertaken for the purpose of both business and pleasure, as well as for the journey through life.

Helps as a talisman to:
- travel safely
- arrive securely at one's destination
- return home safely

Protects as an amulet against:
- highway fever and illness while traveling
- seasickness
- obstacles on a journey

THE RACCOON - *Collector*

The raccoon is the totem animal of playful plenitude. It is constantly busy, storing up food for rainy days, but it always takes time for fun games. It is good at building reserves because it is always aware of itself and what is going on around it. Before eating, the raccoon "washes" its food, that is, prepares it.

Helps as a talisman to:
- take time out for pleasure in spite of much work
- be happy in one's work
- be cautious with one's food and deliberate in its preparation

Protects as an amulet against:
- unemployment
- passion for gambling
- allergies to foods

THE OPOSSUM - *Family*

The opossum worries about its family. It nourishes its young and protects them. With a strong body and spirit, the animal seeks out especially nice places to nest and makes them comfortable. As a totem animal, it provides for harmony in a community.

Helps as a talisman to:
- keep a family together and to nourish it
- create a cozy home
- withstand the many demands of the family

Protects as an amulet against:
- divisions within the family
- potential threats to children
- negligence in family matters

THE BEAR - *Deliberate Action*

The bear has the power of inner vision. In the spring and summer, it searches for honey, which stands for knowledge. In the winter, it hibernates in its cave, letting the events of the year pass by. Sometimes he exerts himself so much during these winter months that he wakes up and is exhausted. He has to sleep a whole other day before re-immersing itself in its meditations. When it finally emerges from its cave in spring, it is brimming with new goals.

Helps as a talisman to:
- "sleep through" one's true intentions and then directly strive for them
- change collected wisdom into deed

Protects as an amulet against:
- waiting too long or inaction
- acting before thinking

THE WOLF - *The Quality of Leadership*

The wolf is a shamanic animal and a highly esteemed teacher, who provides new paths, new ideas, and a new type of thinking. The wolf is a creature of the darkness and loves the moon. This connects to the unconscious. When it howls at the moon, it is partaking in the wisdom and acknowledging its own inner truth.

Helps as a talisman to:
- travel new paths and to rely on one's inner voice
- be at one with the unconscious in the night of the full moon
- learn shamanic rites
- revive aboriginal instincts

Power Animals
of the North American Prairie

Power animals live in the reality beyond. Their being, which lives in the world of our imagination, can affect our daily lives. Each of us has power animals or can acquire them, in order to enhance one's physical or emotional energy and to withstand outside influences. In addition, they endow us with their capabilities so that we make them an essential element of our being.

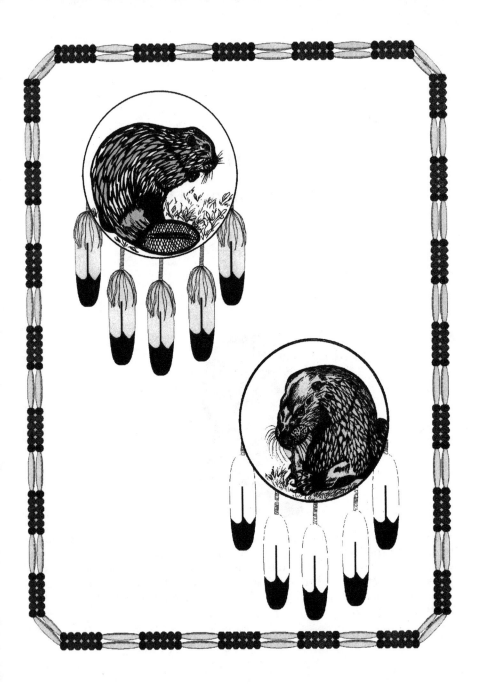

Each of the animals described here can speak to you in a dream or appear in your daydreams. It is also possible to choose a specific animal to aid and protect you with a particular task.

BEAVER - *Chá-pa (l) - Indefatigability*

In different Native American myths, the beaver created the earth out of mud from the ocean floor. In Europe, the beaver is considered the construction engineer, building its dams with tireless energy and diligence. To do this, it has to work together with other beavers.

Helps as a talisman to:
- approach large and small projects eagerly and to do the day's smallest chores with pleasure
- realize ideas and dreams and to be supported by like-minded persons while doing so

Protects as an amulet against:
- not enjoying work
- a wrong approach and waste of energy

RIVER OTTER - *Ptan (l) - Joy of Life*

With grace and playful movements, the otter frolics with its young in the water and on dry land. The otter enjoys life but is also open to others by showing them understanding and by sharing everything with them. It doesn't worry about being taken care of, rather lives for the day and everything that can bring it pleasure.

Helps as a talisman to:
- enjoy life and be happy about other's good fortune
- develop grace and beauty

Protects as an amulet against:
- being bound and enslaved to material goods
- the feeling that life is a struggle

*1 = Lakota (Sioux language)
**n = Navajo

BUTTERFLY - *Kimi'mila (l)* - *Development*

The butterfly belongs to the holy race. It lives through various stages until it rises up into the air as a colorful and luminous creation. It shows us that every transfiguration, even if it is ugly, has its plan. If we follow the plan of the Great Spirit, we too will dance free and beautiful from blossom to blossom like the butterfly.

Helps as a talisman to:
- understand the meaning behind change
- tolerate even the at first glance worthless and to thrill at beauty

Protects as an amulet against:
- the belief that one lives only to work

HUMMINGBIRD - *Love*

This animal is tiny and can fly as it likes; it can even hover. Its long, pointed beak draws nectar from the blossom. Its colorful feathers and buoyant flight make this creature the embodiment of joy and happiness. The hummingbird radiates beauty and love. Huitzilopochtli, the Aztec god of war, and Quetzalcoatl, an important Mayan deity, wore its feathers as a coat because of their magic qualities.

Helps as a talisman to:
- spread and receive joy and luck
- allow beauty to arise and to surround oneself with beauty
- eat for the well-being of body, mind, and soul

Protects as an amulet against:
- situations in which one feels cornered
- anxiety and worry

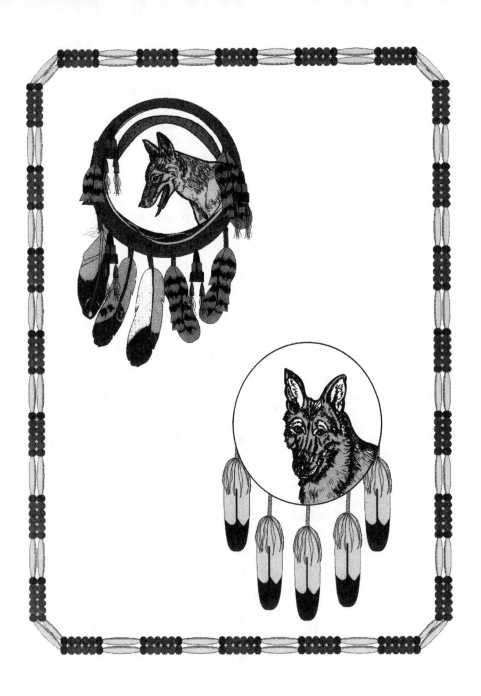

COYOTE - *Ma shle-cha (l) - Ma'ii (n) - Rogue*

The coyote has two faces: one the one hand, he is the creator of the world with all its inconsistencies; on the other hand, he appears to be the rogue, the knave, who wants to outsmart others but often lands on his face. He is always making the same mistakes, because he himself is obviously not able to recognize what can be known. The coyote leads us into situations that are impossible; even so, these experiences help with our development.

Helps as a talisman to:
- not blame others
- laugh about ourselves
- look behind the mirrors by using spells and magic
- see death as a means to eternal life

DOG - *Sun'ka (l) - Fidelity*

He is man's best friend. Before the horse, the Native Americans had dogs, which guarded and cleansed the villages. The dog sets itself apart through its fidelity and steadfast nature. His love for his master exceeds the bounds of life and death. The dog also intervenes in the realm of the dead, making sure that mercy sometimes usurps the law.

Helps as a talisman to:
- take seriously fidelity and devotion
- develop empathy
- keep alert and recognize premonitions so that we can do what is necessary

Protects as an amulet against:
- enemies and attacks

DOLPHIN - *Vitality*

This animal lives in the water but is also a mammal. It is the keeper of breath. The dolphin is the embodiment of the collective conscience. It tells us everything about the We. It does not know an individual personality. It is in tune with the rhythm of life.

Helps as a talisman
- with meditation
- with revitalizing the body's forces
- breathe freely and harmonize with others
- grasp the big picture within a group

Protects as an amulet against:
- choking and drowning

SALMON - *Zealousness*

The salmon seeks out the place of its birth with power and endurance, in order to spawn. He swims against the stream, thinking only of his mission to propagate the species. By seeking out the place of his birth, he is confronted with rebirth and brought into line with his lineage.

Helps as a talisman to:
- return to your ancestors and roots, in order to gain new strength
- consider one's obligations to be natural and to fulfill them dutifully
- swim against the stream from time to time, if the goal calls for it

Protects as an amulet against:
- the danger of being swept along

EAGLE - *Wambli (1) - Healing*

The eagle rises higher in the sky than any other bird. It can see the sun directly. Some Native American tribes believed that the eagle could fly as far as the heavenly houses. It connects us with the Great Spirit and with our own souls.

Helps as a talisman to:
- have visions and to be enlightened
- develop all the qualities of the eagle: strength, courage, endurance, the ability to defend oneself and others, invincibility, speed, agility, the gift of observation, the power of perception, attentiveness
- the full restoration of health

Protects as an amulet against:
- vertigo
- fading in the face of truth

FALCON - *Pisko (1) - Overview*

The falcon is an auger but also a lightning-quick hunter. With its sharp gaze, it pierces the everyday and makes us aware of that which is hidden. Its memory is large, and the falcon can always find examples in its trove of experience to help us in life. From its high perch, it can see dangers as well as good opportunities.

Helps as a talisman to:
- enhance one's power of perception and eyesight, to be more observant
- grab the bull by the horns and turn it to your advantage
- receive an important message
- free one's mind and spirit

Protects as an amulet against:
- myopia
- hesitation

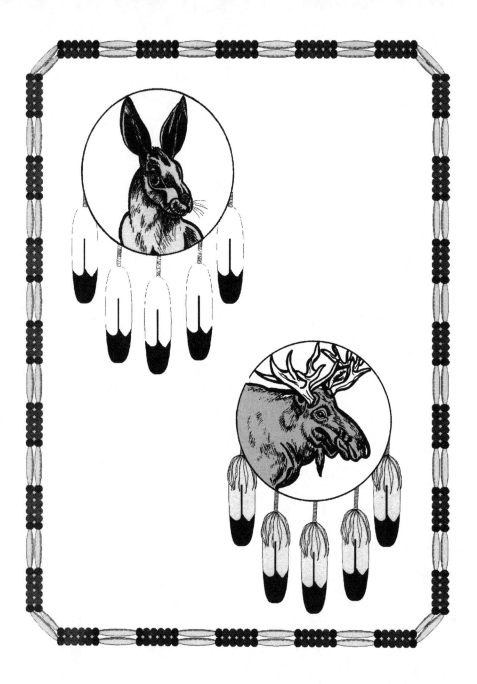

RABBIT - *Tinmastinka (l) - Fertility*

Because the rabbit is so friendly and does not have any weapons, the Great Spirit has given it speed. In addition, it has been granted great fertility, in order to ensure the prolongation of its species. The rabbit is sensitive and easily frightened. A large nose sniffs out danger. It is the example for one's fears coming true. The rabbit is good at hiding and can conceal its young quite safely; the male rabbit is also a good fighter.

Helps as a talisman to:
- be attractive and fertile
- act intuitively and react quickly
- become conscious of the unconscious

ELK - *He-há-ka (l) - Joy of Life*

Without being bothered by the obstacles in its path, the elk charges onward when its loved one calls. Roaring, the elk calls out in joy. It has all the strange qualities of a clan elder and is capable of giving encouragement and support to others. It is a good companion, although sometimes short-tempered. The Sioux associated the elk with the twister or tornado.

Helps as a talisman to:
- form friendships and to keep them
- follow one's heart and to be united with a partner who is one's equal
- be in the possession of courage, endurance, strength, and quickness in stressful situations at work and to thereby win
- share one's happy successes with others

OWL - *Hinhan'sa (l)* - *Clairvoyance*

The owl has different meanings according to the Native American tribe. On one hand, it is honored for its wisdom and its ability to fly at night. It can find lost objects and has healing powers. On the other hand, the owl is uncanny; its cry warns of death and is an ill omen.

Helps as a talisman to:
- recognize the invisible and that which is secret
- develop one's inner sense and intuition
- reveal the intentions of others

RAVEN - *Kangi'tanka* - *Expanding the Mind*

The raven is scintillating and mysterious; its black feathers are like a doorway to infinity. The raven is directly associated with the great spirit, and whoever uses one's own magic to help others can gain healing powers. These powers can even be invoked over broad distances. The raven announces the future so that we can prepare for the necessary changes.

Helps as a talisman to:
- make ceremonies effective and to bring about healing
- go on shamanic journeys
- let go of wrong attitudes and to be enthused about life

FROG - *Gnaska (l) - Purification*

The frog is the messenger of rain. His call tempts the water and cleanses the land. Water purifies the body and the land for the ceremony. The frog's water washes the detritus from the mind and clears up the spirit. We learn about the paths that connect the earthly and divine worlds, and thus, we become shamans. Now we can act as mediums and healers, structuring our surroundings, cleansing places of evil spirits, and freeing the sick from their suffering. Through all this, we have changed our surroundings and ourselves.

Helps as a talisman to:
- free ourselves of ballast and break through the door to the spiritual
- value water as the most important element of our body
- become free and clear
- risk the great leap

TURTLE - *Patkasala (l) - Being Grounded*

Legend has it that the turtle gathered mud on its back from which it created the world. Afterward, it created all living creatures. A power animal, the turtle gives us the necessary grounding to be anchored during our excursions into the spiritual realm. That way, we can return. It also tells us that we don't always have to be in a rush but that strength lies in quiet and caution.

Helps as a talisman to:
- protect one's feelings and to sometimes remain invisible
- have the necessary patience until one matures
- be well-grounded and to feel secure

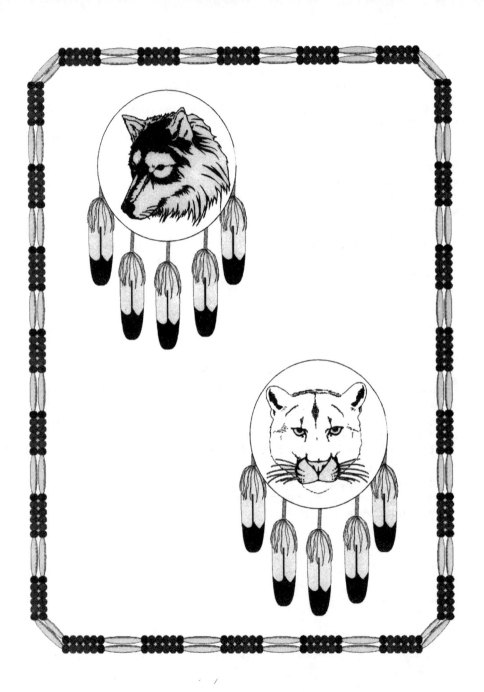

WOLF - *Sunkma'nitu tanka (l) -Teacher*

The wolf is a restless wanderer. It travels the land with speed and returns to his pack with many experiences. The wolf's sense of smell and his instincts are so refined that he can sniff out danger from miles away. It lives in a close relationship to its partner, remaining true all life long. The wolf can teach us to lead a well-balanced life and to have the courage to defend it.

Helps as a talisman to:
- extract ancient wisdom from the unconscious
- stand up for yourself and others
- be attentive and to allow oneself to be led to all that is there

MOUNTAIN LION - *I-gumú-tan-ka (l) - Grace and Strength*

The mountain lion is the born leader, and it understands how to influence situations to its advantage. It needs no one to help or to take up slack for him. The mountain lion is powerful, likes to make decisions, possesses foresight, and is responsible. It attacks instead of retreating. Its sleek nature, ability to make leaps, and well-balanced being make the mountain lion a sovereign spirit, who can teach us to keep our body, mind, and spirit in harmony and teach us to go the way of truth's heart.

Helps as a talisman to:
- take over leadership and to bear responsibility
- enhance one's physical and spiritual dynamism
- discover one's own truth and to follow it without reservation

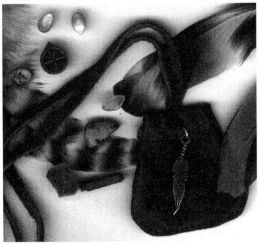

MEDICINE BAG - *Jish (n)* - *Personal Protection*

This bag is worn by North American Native Americans either around the neck or on the belt. There is no medicine bag that is identical with another; each is unique, like its bearer. The bag tells us about its bearer. Even today, young Navajos travel to the four sacred mountains to receive the gift of these stones for the "jish."

We can make or buy a medicine bag for different purposes, filling it with objects that help to fulfill a certain goal. This small sampling should help you to fill your own bag.

In each bag, elements from the animal, plant, and mineral worlds should be present. Reproductions or figurines of animals suffice in the absence of original claws, bones, or hair. Colorful bands of cloth can enhance the magical powers of the bag.

In order to foster and honor the invoked deities place corn, red or white bean seeds, pumpkin, sunflower, or pine seeds in the bag. Some personal offerings enhance the talismanic effect on the medicine bag. This could be a few of your hairs or fingernails. According to Native Americans, the hair is in part the seat of the soul; it brings you into contact with the great spirit.

COLORS

Red	=	Faith
Yellow	=	Vision
Orange	=	Equilibrium
Green	=	Growth, good harvests
Blue	=	Fidelity
Violet	=	Wisdom

COMPASS POINTS

North	=	Wise advice to reach clever decisions
East	=	Enlightenment
South	=	Protection
West	=	Personal truth

ANIMALS

Bear	=	Family, protection of the family and of the young
Beaver	=	Architect, diligence
Buffalo	=	Well-being, plentitude
Coyote	=	Equilibrium, balance, the path of harmony
Lizard	=	Movement, even under difficult circumstances
Falcon	=	Listener, observer
Fox	=	Wit, survivor
Rabbit	=	Vigilance, speed
Deer	=	Interplay of body and soul that leads to health
Horse	=	Inspiration, embodiment of power
Raven	=	Magician; we learn about ourselves and the people around us
Wolf	=	Pathfinder; knows the right way

PLANTS

Apple	=	Passion	Eucalyptus	=	Equilibrium
Jasmine	=	Faith	Lavender	=	Power
Pine	=	Rejuvenation	Rosemary	=	Lifting spirits
Sage	=	Purity	Sandal	=	Harmony
Juniper	=	Concentration	Cedar	=	Soothing

STONES

Agate	=	Courage	Amber	=	Romance
Quartz	=	Lucidity	Hematite	=	Visions
Jasper	=	Well-being	Obsidian	=	Protection
Tiger's eye	=	Courage	Turquoise	=	Healing

BEAR CLAW NECKLACE - *Status and Honor*

The Native American chiefs wore such necklaces made of the claws and the fur of the slaughtered bear. Only the warriors who were wise, brave, and good hunters were chosen as chiefs. The necklace was thus the proof of its wearer's courage and strength in overcoming this powerful animal, whose strength the warrior and hunter later acquired. In addition, the Native Americans believed that the seat of the animal's being was to be found in the claws and bones (and in the horns of other animals). The pearl rosettes are the symbols of the sun and constitute the connection to the great spirit.

BIRD CLAWS WITH STONES

Many Native Americans carried such bird claws with stones. The claws belonged to regal birds such as eagle, falcon, or raven, and endowed the bearer with their powers. The stones had a special significance for the Native Americans, because they were found while seeking a vision or given as a wedding present. The Native Americans associated the specific qualities of the stone with each individual bird, and this accumulated power went over to the bearer, guiding him in the proper ways of the great spirit.

Talismans and Amulets

from Various Cultures and Periods

ASTARTE - *Fertility*

This golden pendant, which was made around 1600 BC in Phoenicia, depicts Astarte, the goddess of love and fertility. The sexual attributes are clearly demarcated- the nipples and the triangle of pubic hair. The pendant was intended to make women sexually attractive and fertile. The gold suggests that a wealthy woman, perhaps a priestess in a temple of Astarte, wore it.

DEVIL'S TRAP - *Good Luck*

For centuries, prayers and incantations have been a part of mankind's life of faith. This includes spells to work good and dispel evil. The adjoining illustration depicts an Assyrian-Semitic "Devil's Trap," which was used some 6000 years ago. The Hebrew text spirals inward, trapping the evil within the bowl; the evil becomes entangled in the coiled writing and cannot escape.

Helps as a talisman to:
- protect against evil and to bring about good luck
- avoid misfortune from the outset
- view evil as something that one can fight and conquer

Protects as an amulet against:
- disaster and danger
- the power of evil

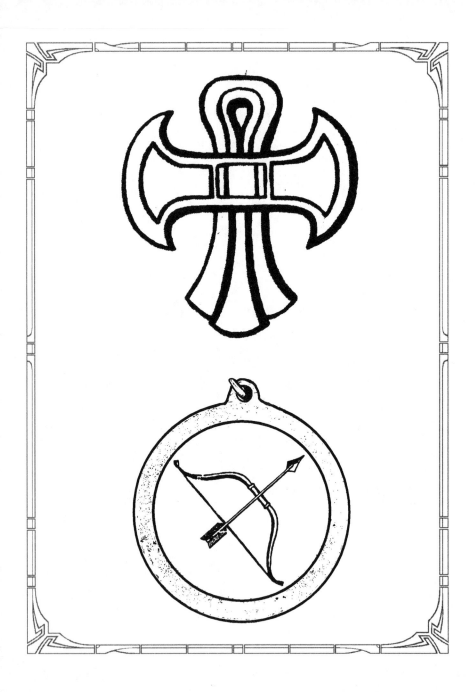

TWO-HEADED AX - *Strength*

The ax shown here is a Cretan two-headed ax. The two halves symbolize the waxing and waning moon, a typically feminine symbol. The ax itself was a status symbol. Thus, the ruler sought to express his connection to the feminine and its source. The two-headed ax has the same meaning in the Near East, the Orient, and Northern Europe. In Hinduism and Buddhism, it is a tool for attaining consciousness and stands at the center of the cycle of birth, death, and rebirth. In China, it is associated with justice, authority, and punishment, and is a symbol of death.

Helps as a talisman to:
- develop strength of character
- become conscious and be just

BOW & ARROW - *Power*

The arrow embodies speed, the bow flexibility. The bow is associated with the moon and is sacred to the goddess of the hunt. The arrow is movement, it stretches beyond borders and is like a ray of sun, making the arrow a symbol of knowledge. The bow is feminine, the arrow male, forming thus the connection to the sensual and to desire, e.g., and cupid's arrows. Shooting with the bow and arrow is a tradition in many Asian cultures. It seeks to free the body of desire: the hand, the arrow, the bow, and the target become one.

Helps as a talisman to:
- overcome egotism
- live in the here and now
- reach the highest being

Protects as an amulet against:
- powerlessness
- aimlessness
- impotence

OM - *The Original Syllable*

Om is the first sound of creation, the breath, which belc
Everything was made in this syllable. It does not belong f
was there before the first words were formed. Through tₙₑ
its proper pronunciation, whole worlds can be created. Steady repeɯɯₑ
leads to deeper meditation and enlightenment. Om stands for the three
states of man: waking, dreaming, and deep sleep.

Helps as a talisman to:
- find peace and quiet
- experience oneself as a part of creation and to unite with the absolute
- experience wordless silence

SRI YANTRA - *Creative Power*

This is the most sacred of all Hindu and Buddhist meditation symbols. It
represents the many levels of consciousness. The male and the female are
united in triangles that point upward and downward. Each of these triangles
stands for a cosmic reality. The triangle motif is framed by lotus leaves, the
symbol of the enlightenment to be attained through Sri Yantra. The four
outer squares are the gateway of knowledge. The spirit of meditation enters
the Yantra through these and gathers in the middle until enlightenment has
been attained at which point it exits through them again.

Helps as a talisman to:
- uncover reality
- be a part of the creative power of the cosmos
- on astral journeys
- demand enlightenment

KUNDALINI - *Vitality*

A person is seated in the lotus position, meditating. The seven chakras (energy centers) and their energy streams are drawn on the body. In the lowest chakra, the power of life (Kundalini) lies rolled up, like a snake. It can be awakened through meditation. It climbs through the chakras up to the skull. As soon as it has reached the cranial chakra, it opens as the thousand-leaf lotus of enlightenment.

Helps as a talisman to:
- arouse one's vitality
- stimulate the chakras
- attain enlightenment

DORJE (BUDDHIST) - *Vajra (Hindu)*

Originally, the thunderbolt belonged to Indra, who used it as a weapon. The two-edged dagger in the middle is a variation on it. Later Shiva used the thunderbolt as a diamond scepter. It thus became a symbol for indestructibility and invincibility. In Buddhism it represents the indomitable male principle. When the thunderbolt on the right is crossed with another, the Vishvavajra arises. This a symbol of the fulfillment of all deeds in every compass direction. The thunderbolt in the middle serves as a nail to pinion demons, who seek to resist the wisdom of the gods. In the Buddhist Dorje (left) one sees traces of a similarity to Thor's scepter (see chapter on Runes).

Helps as a talisman to:
- follow the true path
- not be mislead
- accept one's fulfillment

DRAGON & PHOENIX - *Indivisibility*

Both of these mythical animals are powerful symbols in China, where they represent the power of the royal throne. A dragon stands for the king, a phoenix for the queen. The image of the dragon ensures good luck, prosperity, and divine rain; that of the phoenix for beauty, longevity, and renewal. Together, the symbols represent all the blessings of a long life.

Helps as a talisman to:
- build a wonderful partnership and to enjoy a long life
- climb like the phoenix from the ashes of one's former life and to be happy like a dragon
- begin an indivisible friendship

CHINESE GOOD LUCK SYMBOLS

Bats surround the symbol for luck. In China, the bat brings good luck, because the words for bat and good luck sound alike: FU. Bats live in caves, which are the portals to the beyond. Thus, they are thought to be immortal. When it surrounds a symbol for good luck and a long life, it enhances its power for all time. In Korea, the symbol on the left means joy and happiness. On the right, it stands for longevity or immortality. Sometimes it is represented with other images for a long life. Sometimes it is depicted with other images: with the pine tree or turtle. Placed with a cherry, it wishes a wedded couple to have a long and happy marriage.

Helps as a talisman to:
- bring good luck
- live a very, very long and happy life
- maintain one's health into old age

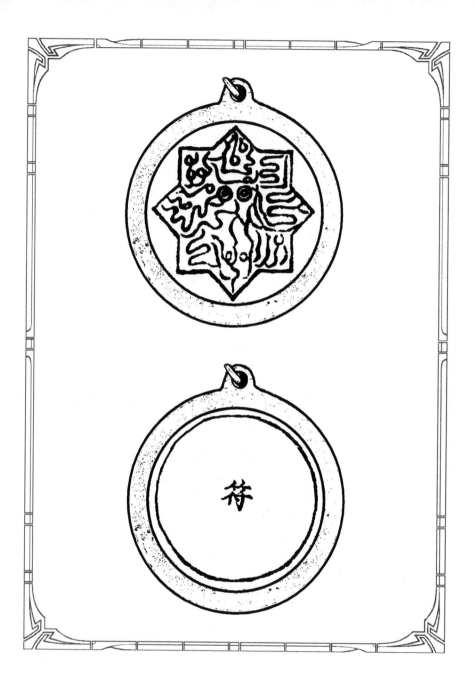

BLACK TALISMAN ON PAPER

The talisman has eight corners, which is a reference not only to water but also to the sacred number eight. In the *I Ching*, the book of changes, there are eight trigrams, which multiplied by themselves create the 64 hexagrams. The talisman is covered with cloud writing, which converges at the center like two eyes. Water and clouds were united by the Taoists as two elements, in order to attain the sought-after harmony.

LARGE CIRCLE TALISMAN

In the art of Taoism, the circle unifies simplicity with perfection, the void with plenitude. The visible and the invisible are joined with each other. The ongoing cycle of eternal return expresses change and movement. In the adjoining talisman, the mystical and philosophical power of this symbol is invoked.

Helps as a talisman to:
- learn the Tao
- go with life's flow and live within its bounds

MITSU DOMO - *Three-way Protection*

The three-pointed swirl (Triskel) can be found in almost all cultures (see Celts chapter). It was probably disseminated by migration. The amulet on the left bears a Japanese Triskel with the names Mitsu Domo. The three interlocking circles represent the course of the sun across the sky: day, dusk, and night. Originally, this symbol was a good luck token, but later it became associated with protection. The smaller illustration on the right depicts a Chinese drum design with the same drawing.

Helps as a talisman to:
- adjust oneself to the course of life
- be happy every day and night

Protects as an amulet against:
- imbalance
- fatigue
- aggressiveness

THE EYE IN THE HAND - *The Hand of God*

Both hand illustrations stem from the Near East and are of Jewish-Arabic origin. They are worn even today as good luck tokens. In antiquity, one concealed one's hands as a sign of respect when meeting a person of higher rank. The open hand represents the intervention of god. The Muslims called this sign Fatima's hand. Fatima was the daughter of the prophet Mohammed. The fingers count as the five pillars of Islam. The hand on the right in the adjoining illustration is of Jewish origin. It is a talisman of strength and power. The hand on the left bears the eye of god, which sees all. This sign is found in almost all cultures. It is a powerful protective amulet.

Helps as a talisman to:
- be powerful and strong
- be in the possession of a powerful belief
- have luck through god's mercy

Protects as an amulet against:
- fear and repression
- misfortune and bad luck

MIMBRES CERAMICS - *Holy Sacrifice*

The Mimbres culture was settled in the southwestern United States and Mexico from 1100 to 1300 AD. It had a strong influence on Anasazi culture. Black was painted on the white ceramic. The illustration shows a four-pointed star, which stands for the four compass points and the medicine wheel. The rest of the picture shows the dance of creation. The pottery was considered sacred and was used for ceremonial purposes. Sometimes the bowls and pots contained the souls of the dead. After the ceremony, the bowls were shattered in order to free the dead souls. Thus, something valuable was sacrificed for a greater good.

Helps as a talisman to:
- complete an honorable project in which one gives away something valuable like time, attention, or love
- give away a beloved possession to please someone else

Protects as an amulet against:
- half-heartedness
- a lack of compassion

MEDICINE WHEEL - *Harmony (hózhó)*

For about 5,000 years, almost all Native American tribes have known a form of the medicine wheel. "Medicine" is the white man's word and does not refer to a medicine one ingests but to the goodness which one can experiences when one engages in these practices. The medicine man is not a doctor in our sense of the term; he is instead a holy man, who communes with the spirits in order to heal. Medicine wheels are constructed around the holy number four, which is a symbol for earth and thus for life. Four represents the four compass points as well as the four elements. The wheel is the symbol of harmony. The adjoining illustration shows a medicine wheel from the southwest. In the middle, one can distinguish the symbols for up and down. Sunbeams emanate from the centerpiece, around which the four elements (fire, water, air, and earth) are arranged. Around the edges stairs depict the ups and downs of life.

Helps as a talisman to:
- develop personal power and equilibrium
- attain wisdom
- follow the rhythm of life and to follow the path of harmony

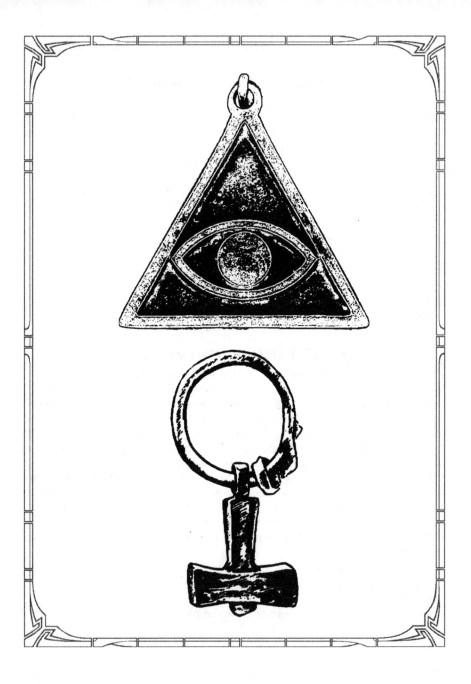

THE EYE IN THE TRIANGLE - *the Evil Eye*

In the cultures of Europe, Asia, and Africa, a belief in the "evil eye" can be found throughout the centuries. The evil eye brings bad luck through the envy and jealousy of another person. Rich, prosperous people were compelled to give money to the poor and not to be cold-hearted. Otherwise, they risked the curse of the evil eye. The gypsies believed that an especially adorable child could be cursed by other mothers. They often gave the children amulets to protect against the evil eye and bad luck. The adjoining amulet reflects evil wishes back to the wisher.

Protects as an amulet against:
- evil wishes
- envy and jealousy
- misfortune

THOR'S HAMMER - *Fury*

Thor flung his hammer away in rage. It struck its mark and returned to Thor. The sparks that it emitted recall the striking of a hammer against an anvil. Whoever possessed a tool in ancient times was highly esteemed. It lent him an aura of power and strength. The god of thunder Thor, also known as the lightning thrower, is comparable to Jupiter, the father of the gods in ancient Rome. His day is Thursday. His hammer was a symbol of power for the northern kings.

Helps as a talisman to:
- achieve social successes
- radiate a powerful presence
- reach one's goal

Protects as an amulet against:
- the petty-mindedness of others
- striking out in the wrong direction
- losses on the stock market

SUN & MOON - *Protection and Well-Being*

On the left, we see the sun in its female form. In certain cultures, the sun was the mother of all life. The emperors of Japan claimed to have descended from the sun goddess Amaterasu. The female sun was life-affirming, warming, and benevolent.

The half-moon with the star, on the right, symbolizes both female and male forces. Together with the star, it depicts here its two conditions: opening and drawing together. In this way, the pendant is a powerful love talisman.

The sun *Helps as a talisman to:*
- be protected

The moon *Helps as a talisman to:*
- be in touch with one's sexuality and well-being

HEART - *Love*

The heart medallion on the left is a classic symbol of love. The picture or a few hairs kept in the heart is a symbolic way of carrying the beloved in one's heart. It is hard to imagine a more beautiful gift of love and friendship. On the right side, a spiral decorates the heart. It points inward, indicating that the journey to self-knowledge leads within, to one's heart. The power of love heals and transforms.

Helps as a talisman to:
- create peace in one's own heart
- feel complete joy
- give and receive love
- be healthy and happy

Protects as an amulet against:
- heart disorders
- lover's anxieties
- the tendency to place blame with others

RING - *Fidelity and Eternity*

The use of the wedding ring goes back to the Romans. The simple ring made of gold represents eternity and the circle of life, because it has neither beginning nor end. A diamond on a gold ring signifies fidelity. The diamond alone stands for hardness, which is why it should always be worn with gold.

The lover's ring in the illustration on the upper far left came into style in the 18th century. On the closed ring, two hands enclose a heart. The meaning is clear: two people who love one another never want to separate. This is reiterated when the ring is disassembled into its five rings, which are inseparably bound to each other.

Helps as a talisman to:
- develop trust in another person
- exhibit one's bond
- cement love and friendship

CLOVER - *Vitality and Happiness*

The three-leafed clover has always been a symbol for vitality because of its vigorous growth. The Celts counted it among their sacred plants. One also finds it in the floor plan of the medieval cathedral. The three-leafed clover symbolizes the trinity. The four-leafed clover is less easy to find. It is a symbol for the good luck upon which one sometimes stumbles. A five-leafed clover, a true rarity, symbolizes a happy marriage.

Helps as a talisman to:
- bring good luck
- enhance one's vitality

INDEX

Abbreviations: (C) = Chinese zodiac; (F) = fetish animals; (P) = power animals; (T) = totem animals; (W) = Western zodiac; Celt. = Celts